FACES I HAVE SEEN

FACES I HAVE SEEN

A MEMOIR OF MURDER

VOLUME II

by

TED JOHNSON

Lulu, Inc.

EDITED BY
Richmond Smith

COPY EDITOR
Victor Flavius

DESIGNED BY
DeAndra Giselle

PHOTOGRAPHY
Sheila Pree Bright

TYPEFACES
Times New Roman, Trajan Pro

PUBLISHED BY
Lulu, Inc.

SPECIAL THANKS TO:
My dear sisters their unwavering love and support cannot be measured in common terms.

Deidra Richardson, my friend forever for reading these stories and having the sincere honesty and charity to tell me her opinion.

Angela Ravin Anderson my loving friend that has been a source of encouragement over the many years of my life.

ISBN 978-1-300-25933-6

To Sara, Iza and Truman my just because...

FOREWARD

After I read this book I had a better understanding of the real Atlanta. I was familiar with the glamorous side you see on television and I had heard references to "the dirty south." But, I didn't know that it was real. In Faces I Have Seen, A Memoir of Murder, Ted takes you on a ride through events that have occurred in Atlanta that caused me to pause and take a look around my environment.

The idea of what I thought an attorney was and the perception of their lifestyle changed. Thus, the realization of the proverbial, don't judge a book by its cover punched me in the mouth. At times, the book would digress to words and phrases commonly used in the vernacular and idiom of the African American Community. But, I was reminded that the content of these stories came from Ted's journal. Thus, I should have expected his thoughts to run together as a stream of consciousness, a surreal dream or an emotional release. Likewise, one does not write in his journal expecting that anyone would ever read or see how he truly feels. To the contrary, Ted has let us inside of his mind.

Ted has exposed himself in this raw, naked expose of his life and career. I was drawn into the stories and the visual accounts of the people that had committed murder and why. I realized the ease of which tragic things can happen that will forever change the course of a person's life and death. Still, I found myself amused as Ted told his stories of murder and intrigued with Ted the person.

Faces I Have Seen, A Memoir of Murder will change the way people will see criminal defense attorneys. Also, I anticipate that this book will humanize the people that are charged with protecting the rights of others. Particularly, for those that find themselves in need of a criminal defense attorney.

Julianne Johnson

CONTENTS

INTRODUCTION 09
Chapter One: Race 19
   The Humility Of Privilege 21
   The Engagement 29
   Niggas In The Valley 37
   Yellow Bitch Syndrome 43
   I Sat Next To The Devil 51

Chapter Two: Oedipus 59
   Computer Love 61
   He's Your Son Not Your Man 69
   Old Spice 79
   Parental Supervision Required 87

Chapter Three: Emasculation 95
   I'm A Man 97
   New Shoes 103
   I'm Just Saying 113

Chapter Four: Identity 119
   Forgiveness 121
   The Citadel 127
   Justice 133
   Measure 139
   Music Man 149

Chapter Five: Friends 155
   Death Of A Birthday 157
   Just Cool 163
   Five O'Clock On Friday 169
   Clean Hands 177

Chapter Six: New Orleans 187
   Who Killed Skinny Pimp 189
   Black 195
   Birthday Wishes 199

INTRODUCTION

SUCCESS

As human beings, our greatness lies not so much in being able to remake the world...as in being able to remake ourselves. -Gandhi

I guess everyone has to answer this question for themselves, "How do I define success?" Most people define success with accomplishments and material wealth. But, I knew I had obtained some level of success when I got the call to interview Ray Lewis, the all pro NFL line backer accused of killing two men at a nightclub after the Super Bowl in Atlanta. My singular accomplishment was that somebody knew my name and someone thought enough of me to call.

I'm almost embarrassed to tell you how I became indecisive about what I should wear to my first visit at the jail. I vacillated between casual and semi formal wear. I wanted Ray to take me seriously. I wanted to look the part of, "I'm a bad man." I wanted to be perceived as a no-nonsense winner. It took me hours to decide what to wear. I was like a little girl preparing for the prom. I wanted to be smaller than what I was. I wanted to have an air about me that exuded appeal, competence and confidence. I wanted Ray Lewis to believe in me. Ray being accused of double murder killing someone's son and father was just an afterthought.

My whole life flashed before me. I remembered all the negative shit people had said about me and laughed. I screamed to myself, "Look at me now you motherfuckers" and in my mind, they did. In my mind everyone saw me. After this, I would be known as the guy that represented Ray Lewis. I was so proud of myself. I have habitually placed little value in what people thought of me because I know at their core, most people ain't about shit. So, I decided as a child to define myself in spite of the fact my own daddy told me I was a fool.

Like a smitten little girl, I had a million questions for the caller that turned out to be Ray's uncle. How did you find out about me? Who referred you? What did they say? I had to be sure to temper my questions. I didn't want anyone to think that it was my first time.

In fact, it wasn't the first time that I gotten a referral from out of state but certainly, I had never represented anyone of Ray's celebrity status. I mean there was Left-Eye of the R&B singing group. I was good enough to represent the people in her production company. But when she burned down her ex-beau's house, the NFL player, she hired a female Jewish attorney. Like most black folks with money, she didn't trust me to represent her. So, I quit representing her folks. And, of course, I did not return their retainer.

However, like most prideful black attorneys I refuse to accept my second class status because I understood the second class mentality of black people. This is not to say, that black attorneys just market themselves to black folks. Some blacks think that Mr. Charlie can do more for them than I can. Even if blacks are forced to hire black lawyers, they somehow think that the services provided are less than those who are non-black. They mistakenly think that there is a sentimental component to the representation because we're all black. I got a feeling that Ray was going to be different.

My reputation had traveled all the way to Baltimore. My name floating around in celebrity circles, I'm feeling quite successful today. Reflecting back on my life, I'm a long way from the dry cleaning class I took through high school coupled with lunch and gym, which completed my school day. I'm a long way from the Southside of Indianapolis, Indiana, from the factories and the sulfur emissions from Eli Lillie's Pharmaceuticals that polluted the water and air.

Yes, my name was floating around in high cotton now. So, I got in my car and drove to see Ray. I decided to wear my East Coast garb which included my black tweed derby cap, black V-neck sweater and white Oxford button down. I wore my Cole Haan loafers and jeans; it was an after hour Monday visit. I thought that I was casually cool for the occasion. It was late, so the need to wear a suit was a bit over the top.

Ray didn't have to know that last Friday I rode around with Walter in his pickup truck. We waited in the parking lot of a Church's Chicken for nearly an hour for some money. Thereafter, Walter took me to another client's house and we waited out of view around the corner for my client to come home. As the client approached his door, Walter and I approached him for my fees that had been earned. As he paid me, he asked, "What kind of lawyer are you?" I told him "One that would make house visits for my money."

The client was clearly under the impression that I was there to take my money if he wasn't prepared to give it to me. Perhaps, I was. Both, Walter and I are as dark as the night, 6'3" and over 250 pounds. I figured that I wouldn't have to tell Ray about my successful career. Besides, my collection practices with other clients were privileged information. The important fact, Ray would be able to pay.

I told Walter that I was going to stop this shit one day of driving by houses; waiting in parking lots and strip clubs to get paid. This going out on a limb putting him in harm's way to collect my money was not cool. Even, though, on occasions I'd ride with him to do the same thing. But unlike him, I didn't have kids. Walter told me that the fruit was on the limb. We could wait for it to fall to the ground or we could pick it off the tree. Walter said I looked like I had waited long enough. Before we laughed. At the time, I was hungry and broke.

I pondered, "What should I charge Ray two hundred and fifty or three hundred thousand dollars?" It doesn't matter that I routinely charged ten to twenty thousand for the run-of-the-mill-murder, and people typically needed a payment plan to pay that, but this was Ray Lewis. At the time, I didn't think this was price gouging, most lawyers' fees depend on who they're representing and what they think a client can pay. Thus, if you walked in the office carrying a Prada bag you got a Prada quote. Likewise, if you were carrying a knock off Gucci bag, you still got a Prada quote because I sensed your ambition.

The drive over to the jail took me about thirty minutes. I checked into the jail and filled out the necessary Requests For Visit forms. The deputies working the desk smiled at me with thoughts of validation, as they read Ray Lewis' name on my form. Doing such a mundane task every day, it gets exciting when a high profile case comes through the jail. The media trucks parked outside waiting to get the scoop to air as breaking news at 11.

Today was my day and I like most, defined success as goal obtainment that evidenced itself with material wealth. I was not above playing into the perception of things leaving the substance hidden as my business. Typically people don't walk around professing how fucked up they are. At least, I didn't. I carried myself as a Hitter. A criminal defense attorney that would fight to the bitter end to get a verdict my way and would run through almost anything to get what I wanted.

When it came to my work and life, I had enough passion that people could touch and break-off a little piece for themselves. Yes, my passion was tangible and it had color. If you were around me long enough it could rub off and it was contagious. A passion that could get a strangers panties wet thereby rebuking the monotony she's left at home. A reality bogged down by stress choking any hope of her dreams for an enjoyable life. I had a passion worth paying for.

I figured that's why Ray's folks called me. Obviously, I had been successful at portraying the perception of success and someone bought it. Understandably, I did my part to solidify my image. I understood very early on that my whole image would have failed had I not won my share of murder cases. More importantly, I understood how I wanted people to see me and I assisted them by portraying that very image.

As the deputy approved my request for visit, folks in the lobby of the jail and deputies alike were coming out of the woodwork to see me. They wanted to see the guy that would represent Ray Lewis charged with what has now been coined "The Super Bowl Murders." The jail has a long corridor that led to the elevators. In Atlanta, people charged with murder are usually kept on the seventh floor and that was my destination. My walk down the corridor to the elevators seemed to take longer because in my imagination, I was walking through the crowd as people patted me on the back and congratulated me. I was Ray's lawyer. In reality, there were no pats on the back and people were walking slowly because the floors were recently buffed by inmate Trustees and were thus, slippery.

As the elevator took me up to the seventh floor, Ray was sitting there waiting for me. I told him that his uncle had called me and wanted me to advise him on his situation. I introduced myself and went into my spiel, which included how good and experienced I was. I essentially repeated to him what I had heard on the news. Ray was polite and quiet as he listened attentively. As I spoke, Ray sat patiently to allow me to finish. In my mind we talked for hours but in reality it was a good two minutes before Ray told me; "I've already hired a lawyer", and thanked me for coming down. Ray had consulted with another black attorney who had referred Ray to an older white guy. The white guy's reputation was that he was just the baddest motherfucker in-town with thirty years of experience, and he was.

After my experience with Ray, I had to redefine my definition of success. I had to trade my old definition in for a new one. Life in many ways has forced me into this position. Seemingly, I will never have the shit that goes along with my first definition of the word success, material wealth. To the contrary, it's much easier for me to say, "I don't need it," to the approval of others who are similarly situated. Likewise, I think I'll just define success as the ability to do what makes me happy. Travel, eat good food, drink brown liquor and entertain beautiful women. Hence, as Mother-Nature and Father-Time conspire on my libido, I reserve the right to redefine success for myself in the future.

I told Mr. Benny about my experience with Ray. Mr. Benny and his wife owned the shoe repair shop around the corner from the federal courthouse. I think Mr. Benny knows that I come to him when I have shit on my mind. From somewhere in the mid-west, Mr. Benny had to be in his late fifties or early sixties. His wisdom is barely tempered by his impatience with foolishness. "Get in the chair now and watch your step." "Don't let that cell phone get you killed." "Ain't no need for my insurance to go up cause of your negligence." I think Mr. Benny had done some federal time, but he's not the type to share it with you. I've been coming to Mr. Benny over six years now and he keeps me in step with myself.

I told Mr. Benny that I almost had Ray signed up but I lost him. I don't know how he knew, but Mr. Benny told me that he had heard I had interviewed Ray. He then told me that success is a road traveled up hill and I hadn't been here long enough for the powers that be to allow me to have such a case, but if I stayed long enough and kept my nose clean, one was coming. I took heed to Mr. Benny's advice. He's the shoe repairman that knows shit you don't think he should. As he shined my shoes, I sat quietly and reflected on the message he had just given me.

For a few hours, I became delusional and consumed in my self-importance. I must say, it felt good. I felt the euphoria of walking around with the winning lottery ticket in my pocket. Then, to have the feeling of that moment drowned by an episode of momentary impotence, when you've learned you didn't win. Hence, a day that in an instance started out bright and sunny, but ended in patchy drizzle. I tell myself, I'm not getting off my high horse. We have enough people in the world that are afraid to ride.

Although, I had the reflection one confronts, when he's learned he didn't win. At least, I tried to play. Yeah, anyone that knows me knows that I did. They know that I like a good game. Thus, in my mind's eye, even if I were to go blind today, I can see the sun and it's all right. I gladly paid Mr. Benny his money.

Today, I'm sure that Ray doesn't know or remember me from Adam. I'm probably one of many attorneys that came to visit him that Monday talking the same old shit I put down. Even, more, I'm sure that whole "Super Bowl Murder" experience is something Ray's tried real hard to forget. But for a day, one Monday evening, Ray allowed me to know what it meant to feel successful and it felt good.

During Ray's murder trial, which quietly became a circus broadcasted all over the country, Ray pled guilty to a misdemeanor and a two hundred and fifty thousand dollars fine. Thus, Ray spent no time in jail. Also, Ray's two co-defendants were found not guilty of murder. People said that Ray paid the old white guy $1 million dollars in attorney fees. But, you know how folks talk. Had Ray gone with me, I would have given Ray the old sentimental bargain.

CHAPTER ONE

RACE

HUMILITY OF PRIVILEGE

S arge thought that his uniform gave him privilege over others that didn't wear a police uniform to work. He knew that the uniform was the only thing that gave him any credibility in the world and he chose to use it to his advantage. Sarge would use his uniform to enter the stadium or arena for free professional basketball and football games. He would even flash his badge to get free access to nightclubs so he could party. After getting away with his shit for so long, Sarge's abuses became more and more egregious. The shit hit the fan on Sarge when he kept taking pussy and not paying for it.

Most people try to respect people in position of authority even if they live a life of crime. Deep down inside, most people want to trust the police and law enforcement in general. Having worked with cops for most of my life, I know that cops can be some of the most frustrated people on earth. I mean not many of us go to work with the presumption that a motherfucker may shoot at us or kill a co-worker. In our off-time, many of us don't have to worry about the stress of encountering a person we've arrested and upon seeing us, he wants to cut the fool. Thus, the one-time suspect has no respect for the cop in this cops and robbers world we live in.

However, Sarge was on some other shit because he was corrupt from the beginning. I can't say that I was any better as a person than Sarge. But, I'd like to think that I would take shit because I was hungry. Sarge was the type that would quench his thirst and hunger and take a bag of shit with him for later. I would characterize Sarge's behavior as stealing because he took more than he needed. On the other hand, I would consider my behavior as satisfying a basic need. Like many, I'm full of these contradictions. I know that there are those that would consider Sarge and I thieves. But, at least they'd say that I only took what I needed. To the contrary, Sarge was the smart or greedy one depending on your perspective.

Those that live a life of crime just want to operate in their world out of sight from the authorities. But, authorities are paid to find them and it ain't hard to find the pimp you grew up with still working the same neighborhood. Like most merchants, a criminal doesn't mind giving a little extra to a repeat customer but at some point the freebies cut in to the profit margin and certain practices have to change. However, Sarge felt that change wasn't applicable to him because he was the law.

Humility of privilege is a rare occurrence. It takes a special person that has the benefit of life treasures to share them with those that have less. We just put Mr. Charles in the ground. He was one of those privileged people that had humility. Mr. Charles died right after he represented the Southern Christian Leadership Conference "SCLC" the very organization that Dr. Martin Luther King Jr. himself and Dr. Joseph Lowery started.

The SCLC leadership started stealing from the coffers and something had to be done. Mr. Charles litigated for the good side for several months. Martin's daughter Bernice was his client and Mr. Charles prevailed for her interest. After which, Bernice declined the leadership she and the SCLC had begged Charles to obtain. The very leadership that Bernice claimed she had wanted to further her daddy's work and legacy. Sadly, Mr. Charles was never appropriately paid for his time and skill. The stress he endured associated with folks fighting over money and power was overwhelming in itself. Months later, Mr. Charles was dead. Some say that Mr. Charles had worked himself to death.

Mr. Charles lived in a Buckhead mansion on a hill down the street from the Governor. He had a successful law practice that brought him millions and yet he allowed the less fortunate into his home. Every attorney in Atlanta wanted to be invited to Mr. Charles's Christmas party. We knew we weren't shit if we weren't invited to the party. Mr. Charles would put out the crystal wine glasses and champagne goblets for our pleasure. Lamb, Pâté and cheese platters abounded with beautiful young servers at your beck and call. With some partygoers knowing that it was their turn to clean the chittlins at Christmas. The party was a time to feel a part of something of social importance.

At one of Mr. Charles's parties, I saw Maurice Benoit dance all of the sugar out of his tank. The power of Maurice was that he didn't give a shit of what anybody thought of him. He was good looking, smart and a successful international attorney himself. Maurice told me once that if I'd lose my stomach I would be all right. I knew Maurice was fucking with me as he pinched the side of my belly.

When I worked in Chicago, Phillip with his Tom Selleck mustache and Barry White perm that fell to his shoulders got me too. I recall how I was feeling quite smug that December day wearing my indigo blue Armani suit, crispy white shirt and skinned cowboy boots. As I walked into the courthouse cafeteria with my dick swinging underneath my suit; Phillip was sitting with a group of women and in my delusion of grandeur; I knew they had to be talking about me.

Phillip in his feminine yet baritone voice asked me if I knew what he wanted for Christmas. I knew the question was a set up. In fact, the women at the table had already begun to laugh. I said no Phillip, "What do you want for Christmas." Phillip retorted, "I want some pussy from you." The room erupted into full hysteria. I must say, it was funny as hell. Shortly, thereafter, I moved to Atlanta. I never saw Phillip again; I heard he had died of complications from AIDS. The last time I saw Maurice, he had imposed himself on Walter

Robinson, my running buddy and I, as we lunched at the Busy Bee; a soul food restaurant in the Westend of Atlanta. Maurice felt that he could sit with us because we were cool like that. When our friend Moses' died Maurice was one of the few that gave significantly to the trust fund we had set up for Moses' kids. Now, Maurice in all of his fabulosity is gone too.

At Mr. Charles parties, it was funny to see how these black folks merely high school years away from their mommas walking around on the back of an old pair of shoes and in need of several safety pins to hold up her house coat enjoying life as it could be for them. I would watch these partygoers holding these expensive crystal glasses like mason jars filled with sugary Kool Aid.

In spite of our lack of couth, Mr. Charles knew our asses were dragging, but allowed each of us in and showed us how to dream. At one of his parties, I recalled sipping on some buttery white wine with a floral bouquet that one of the servers had given me to taste. I swirled it around in my mouth thinking if momma's insurance man could see me now. He used to look at me like I wasn't gon be shit, when I'd tell him that "Momma said she wasn't home and to come back next week if he wanted to get paid."

After I sampled the wine, I gave her the nod to keep pouring and told her to stay close as I grabbed a handful of those little tooth-picked sausages in my cocktail napkin. The server looked at my country ass with the left eye of suspicion, but she really had no idea just how country-ghetto I was and proud of it.

Mr. Charles's party allowed the black attorneys in attendance to self-evaluate and to learn how to get our asses off the ground. At the same time, Mr. Charles allowed the white attorneys to re-evaluate doing business with black attorneys. Thus, killing the stereotype that most black attorneys are only equipped to handle black clients and its okay for blacks and whites to work together. Because at the end of the day, we all wanted to be like Mr. Charles and make some money.

Privileged but with the humility of a person that understood the importance of another man having a dream. At his funeral, everybody black, white, Jew, gentile, men, women, ministers, cops, politicians and other lawyers claimed that Mr. Charles was their best friend because he had simply and unselfishly shared his life with us.

To the contrary, Sarge wanted to keep those he felt that was beneath him down because he wore a uniform, a uniform that was supposed to represent integrity, honesty and courage. For Sarge, his uniform was used to take free pussy from those he felt wasn't in position to holla about it, until Moonie got tired. Moonie had been pimping since high school and he was known to pitch a little dope to make ends meet. On a few occasions, Moonie had given Sarge a pass on the free pussy but enough was enough. Moonie figured what kind of man was he to allow anybody to just take his shit for free. It was the principle of the whole thing.

Sarge dressed in plain clothes with his badge bouncing off of his chest went over to Moonie's trap and was solicited by a fat white girl. They came to terms and Sarge did what he had come to do and told the prostitute "Get your fat stanky ass out of my truck." Prior to Sarge's arrival, Moonie had told the prostitute to just go to jail if Sarge came back over there looking for some free pussy and she was prepared to go. However, at gunpoint, Sarge repeated his instruction to her, "Get your fat stanky ass out of my truck." The prostitute called Sarge a corrupt nigga and insisted that he was going to pay for the pussy. When Sarge refused, the prostitute called for Moonie and he came running with his gun in his hand.

By all accounts, Moonie knew his girl was turning a trick for Sarge before she called for him. Seemingly, Moonie had been waiting on Sarge's return. As Moonie approached the area where the sex had occurred, he and Sarge made eye contact when shots were fired. Moonie was fatally struck underneath his arm as he had raised it to fire on Sarge. Sarge then jumped out of his truck and took cover beside it. The truck shielded Sarge from Moonie and his people. However, Sarge knew there was only one way in the trap and one way out. He also knew that there were some woods that separated that apartment complex from the other, so Sarge ran for the woods. Within minutes, police were on the scene.

Police arrested Sarge as he attempted to climb over a ten-foot tall fence into the neighboring complex. Sarge pulled out his badge and told his fellow officers that he was one of them. Thus, the investigation immediately became one to account for the shooting as one done in self defense and not murder. Police figured that Sarge could explain the free pussy part some other time. People get upset when police look after their own but everyone does it. So, why shouldn't they?

When Sarge retained me, I convinced the Diva to give him a bond. The Diva is an Atlanta legend. She was the first black female Superior Court judge in the state of Georgia. As you know, Georgia was one of the original thirteen colonies in America, so her being chief judge was reason to celebrate. The Diva wore her long pretty black hair to her shoulders, which perfectly accented her caramel brown complexion. The Diva's make-up, polished nails and sweet perfume was all indications that she had groomed herself for hours before she left the house. The Diva even spoke with an English accent even though she was from Chicago. I guess her perfect diction was a carryover from her days as a school teacher.

I informed the Diva that Sarge was a childhood friend of Walter Robinson. I had Walter to testify at Sarge's bond hearing that he was not a threat to himself nor was he a threat to other people. I knew that the Diva loved Walter like a son and respected him as a young father with daughters. Walter was a local attorney that grew up with Sarge in Southwest Atlanta. A former NFL football player and the son of a female evangelist, Walter would go into convenient preacher mode, when he would attempt to appeal to a Christian for leniency.

One of Walter's favorite past times was to lure unsuspecting folks into philosophical debates about the racial identity of Christ. As if, Christ ethnicity made a difference to those looking to be saved. Walter stood at least 6'3, with a stump football neck and massive shoulders. Walter would speak with a religious conviction if he would speak about anything, which always gave the conversation a sense of urgency.

The state told the Diva how Sarge had converted his private motorcycle into an official police motorcycle look-alike, and was going around town stopping folks illegally. Ironically, the District Attorney accused a cop of impersonating a cop. Knowing that information, I knew the Diva would not be so inclined to release Sarge. So I had to confess to the Diva that Sarge was suffering from AIDS. He was HIV positive and in need of medical cocktails to stay alive. Thus, the taxpayers could pay for his treatment or Sarge would be responsible for himself upon his release. The Diva gave Sarge a bond but one she knew he couldn't make and pay me. After a few years, Sarge chose to spend his money and get out of jail on bond.

I can't substantiate whether Sarge was a serial rapist or not as he cruised about town on his fake motorcycle while in uniform, but I do know that he got some bad pussy from somewhere. However, Walter was under the belief that Sarge was a switch hitter. In his twenties, a strong, young, athletic Sarge did provide security for Elton John, a part time resident of Atlanta. But, I don't know if Sir Elton was the type to fuck the help. It seems that he would have too much to lose and besides, if he did, Sarge would not have trouble paying for my services. He did, so I quit.

The Public Defender's Office picked Sarge's case up and almost ran him to victory. During the first trial, the jury could not decide on a verdict so they had to retry Sarge on the murder charges. During the trial, I was told that the fat white prostitute didn't know her own birthday or age. Also, the folks from the complex where the shooting occurred testified that they were so happy somebody killed Moonie's ass that they had a party. Moonie had terrorized their community for so long, no love was loss in his passing. Somebody was bound to kill Moonie, why not the police even if he had taken the pussy and didn't pay for it.

Unfortunately for Sarge, the second jury convicted him of voluntary manslaughter and the judge sentenced him to prison. For Sarge, it was as if the judge signed his death warrant for he will not receive the medical care he would receive on the outside. I guess the lesson for Sarge was the cost he paid for the free pussy was too much. Sarge abused his privilege to serve and protect his community. To help somebody in a positive way, to be more like Mr. Charles.

The humility of privilege to serve and help somebody. Oh, they may not know that you've helped them but you will. And I promise you, you'll feel good about it and when you die people will say that you were their best friend and GOD will hear them. GOD will ask Saint Gabriel, "What manner of man was he, who stands at my gate?" Saint Gabriel will answer "he was a good man of privilege and humility. He brought many to you and he helped those that needed help in your name."

Now, Sarge, what manner of man was he? Sarge will have to answer for himself. I imagine Moonie will be screaming from the top of his lungs from the bowels of hell to the good Lord, that's the nigga that killed me! And you know what, GOD will hear him.

Sentence: *Voluntary manslaughter twelve years to serve in prison.*

THE ENGAGEMENT

I asked Sheila again and again, the same questions, you were intoxicated at the time of the incident weren't you? I challenged and encouraged her to feed into the stereotype that all black people look alike to her. Finally, I asked her if she were sure that things happened to her the way she claimed they did. Hence, through her tears, frustration and angst, she said they had. The more Sheila cried the harder I pushed, I wasn't going for the sentimental white woman crying bit that they used throughout history. I told myself that was same bit that got Emmett Till and so many others killed and imprisoned.

At the time, I was as insensitive as a poisonous snake. I bit because I could and not because I felt threatened. I bit because I could do it and get away with it. My badgering went beyond just seeking the truth. For some reason, I made it personal and everyone in the room could tell. I went on and on for what seemed to be hours before the prosecution objected to my badgering and the court agreed and sustained the objection.

Thereafter, I continued again with the same questions with a different twist for the hell of it. Looking back on it, I didn't expect her answers to change. It wasn't like I was looking for a Perry Mason moment. It was more like I had nothing better to do and I didn't feel like sitting my adversarial ass down. Even though, there was no point to be made, she identified my client Clyde Pierce as the person that shot her fiancé, Donald Rathbone; as Clyde and another attempted to rob them.

One day in 1983, Clyde and Jefferson Smith were cruising through Buckhead, which is a high rent district in North Atlanta. The two were looking for someone, anyone to rob for a few dollars. Clyde had just been released from prison less than two years ago for a prior armed robbery when this incident occurred. Being in the early to mid-eighties, ATM cash machines were becoming more vogue and the crime element was trying to figure out ways to exploit the machines or people that had access to them. Hence, people with bank accounts and for Clyde and Jefferson that meant white folks. At the time, affluent white folks were known to be in Buckhead.

Thus, robbing crews and teams of thieves abounded across the country with a rash of stickups and mayhem at ATM's, when these two niggas got caught. A friend had turned them in for the reward money. Clyde and Jefferson were sentenced to life in prison plus 10 years for the armed robbery and murder of Donald Rathbone. However, their cases were reversed on appeal because Clyde and Jefferson were represented by the same lawyer in a capital murder case. This was a procedural no- no in the more sophisticated world in the late 1990's. So this time around, I was appointed by the court to represent Clyde.

Like most clients charged with murder, I first met Clyde at the county jail. He appeared to be nearing fifty years old or better. He had smooth black skin, which I thought was odd for a man imprisoned for nearly the last twenty years. Moreover, Clyde had a Fu Man Chu style mustache, shaved head and 3 inch long fingernails on every finger. When I would interview Clyde, he'd clean his nails with the same hand. He kept his head titled upward during the interview as if he held me under suspicion.

Ammad Patel was a lawyer in waiting and my assistant at the time. Patel was from India, Americanized and accent free. Patel had an almost innocent curiosity about people, which fascinated me about his culture. I first met Patel, when he was an intern at the Public Defender's Office. He became my assistant after he finished law school, as he studied for the bar exam. Patel reminded me of the prototype Americanized Indian man. He was not very tall, slender but not too skinny like the men in India. Patel was at least second generation American and had lost the accent long ago if he ever had one. You couldn't tell he was of Indian decent over the telephone.

Patel wore nice suits, Armani or Boss usually in dark colors. It was apparent that Patel was ingrained in American professional protocol and he had his own style to prove it, which was not only fashionable but cool. I would sit back and observe how Patel and Clyde would interact. I don't think Clyde had ever encountered an Indian man outside a convenience store. Let alone, one that spoke better English than the both of us.

In Chicago, I had worked with Rami Davi, a man of Indian decent at the State's Attorneys' Office. Rami had attended a prestigious school in Washington D.C. Rami was as dark as me with this rich wavy hair. His credentials were top notch but he stilled appeared to be pensive if not flat out nervous around white folks. When we were together, I got the impression that he would change when white folks came around.

I would observe, as Rami tried real hard to fit in but his heavy accent didn't make it easy for him. I began calling Rami "Stan the Teflon Man", and he would ask why. I told Rami, with his ability to be so agreeable with everybody that nothing could stick to him; much like Teflon. He didn't understand that I was suggesting that he stood for nothing. I couldn't tell Rami how I quietly resented how he would kiss white folks' asses. And on the other hand, have empathy for his internal confusion in how he wanted to be accepted and perceived.

Unlike, Rami, Patel acted like a privileged white boy and was comfortable in his own skin. Patel had the nuts to disagree with shit he didn't agree with and have an honest opinion why. I enjoyed Patel's candor and innocence. In some ways, the purity of his positions kept me honest and pushed me away from my position, that most people ain't shit. Thus, Patel's innocence trumped my cynicism and the rebirth of giving folks the benefit of the doubt. On the contrary, Rami just wanted acceptance more than he needed respect.

Being one of the few ghetto boys on my college basketball ball team that consisted of guys from upper crust backgrounds, I knew what Rami was going through. I knew that my teammates laughed at my short comings behind my back and took odds on whether I would even graduate or amount to shit. Also, there was Billy Bob, a white guy considered as poor white trash. They also had tight faces when it came to accepting Billy Bob. But, Billy and I were from Indiana. We understood their attitudes about us, but it didn't stop shit. Billy and I knew we didn't come from much, but what we did have was staying power. Being as hungry as we were for a better life, they had no idea who we really were.

My college basketball coached vowed that I would never graduate, so long as he was the coach. He told me that there were more deserving white folks than me that should benefit from the Institute. Coach swore that his statements were made with the best of intentions. After all, he wasn't a racist; he was married to a black woman.

Little did he know, after making such a statement, I would die trying to graduate. My aunt used to wash the sheets at the Institute before women and blacks were allowed to attend. The motherfucker didn't know that he had just given me another reason matriculate from the Institute; it was now personal. But in my arrogance, I never tried to fit in because I could not deny that my dad worked at the rubber plant that their fathers could own. My strength was that I knew who I was at a time when they were still hiding behind their dad's name afraid to fly. I also understood, why fly alone when your daddy was so willing to carry you.

I never told Rami my story to help him with his. I just hoped that he would get it that those that care too much about accepting you as a friend really aren't sure who they are. And in most cases, they should be so lucky. Sometimes, when you knock the rust off and apply a little grease, some things can work forever, like friendship. However, Rami would have to learn these life lessons like everyone else, through personal experience.

As we progressed through the case together, Clyde's rapport with Patel grew. Patel's questions to me and then to Clyde were sincere and honest. As with most people, who sort through the cultural differences and find the boundaries for honest conversation. Patel wanted to know if Clyde had anything to do with Mr. Rathbone's murder. Since Clyde denied involvement, Patel wanted to help him. Apparently, Clyde knew that his sincere denial to Patel didn't mean shit to me. Thus, we engaged in one word conversations for weeks before I stopped trying.

I would ask Clyde, what's up, how are you doing? Clyde would respond, fine. I would ask, do you have any questions of me? Clyde would respond, no. I'd ask him about Jefferson and his involvement with Mr. Rathbone's murder? Clyde's response would be, "what?" I'd say, what my ass before I would pack my files up and leave. I admit that I would leave Clyde's ass in the interview room because he was not going to waste my time nor was he going to control me.

Thereafter, I would send Patel to interview Clyde on future visits. One day Patel returned to the office and told me Clyde wanted to plea bargain. For Patel, it seemed as if it were the first time someone had lied to him. However, I knew that it was not the first time Patel had sat in the presence of a murderer. Patel just wanted to believe in Clyde and Clyde knew he had let Patel down. Patel had learned what most women go through when they fall for the wrong man. At least, Patel didn't have to fuck him before he found out Clyde wasn't shit but a stick up boy.

Sheila told the jury that twenty years ago, Rahtbone had gotten a contract that would change his life, their life together. They got engaged and decided to move in together into this beautiful Buckhead apartment. Rathbone was from an affluent background, but by all accounts, he didn't want to live off his daddy's money. He wanted to make his own. Just in his thirties, Rathbone's life was about to take off. The movers were coming or had just left, but in the mean time, the couple decided to sip champagne and celebrate new beginnings.

The couple had brought some personal items to the apartment in their respective cars and would retrieve the same in between sips of champagne. As they casually removed items from their cars, Sheila decided to take a break and sat on a stoop outside of the apartment building, when she was approached by Jefferson and Clyde. Sheila knew immediately that they were asking her bullshit questions before guns were drawn and she was accosted. Sensing something was wrong, Rathbone came outside to check on his soon to be bride when he encountered the two men. Clyde told Rathbone to be cool. He just wanted his wallet. Rathbone charged at Clyde as he told Sheila to run. A single shot to the chest. Rathbone was dead.

Sheila cried as she testified, I guess seeing Clyde and being in Court again for this shit was too much. I mean how many times was she to relive it because the state was too cheap to give these crooks their own lawyers. I don't know why Sheila never remarried but I could guess. I don't know if anyone wants to live a life as a widower or if anyone truly wants to be alone. I've been alone before and I could never handle the silence.

I badgered every witness the state presented from over twenty years ago. The state even found old William Jones the man that got the reward money for calling the police. Jones told the jury that he knew it was Clyde that killed the man in Buckhead. He identified the hat he saw on the 6 o'clock news. Jones said that Clyde wore a hat just like the one he saw on the news, inscribed with the words "bait & tackle" with an anchor symbol separating the words. I flippantly, retorted to Jones, that the manufacturer made more than one hat. Jones agreed, but he knew that the hat belonged to Clyde after Jefferson told him how the white man slapped it off of Clyde's head during their struggle over Clyde's gun. Jones stated as he did twenty years ago, that Jefferson's confession was good enough for him. Jones opined only a fool or a hurt lover confesses to murder. Even more, Jones never said whether Jefferson was just a fool or something else.

I asked Sheila, again and again, you were drunk as hell when you were accosted by two black men? Isn't it true, that all black men look alike to you? Before this incident, you had never seen this man a day in your life. Sheila patiently agreed with all of my questions until I asked her, how are you so sure that Clyde was one of the men that accosted you and killed Rathbone. Sheila replied, because that was the day a little bit of me died with Donald. At least, in my heart, that's what I heard.

The jury didn't take long to convict Clyde for a second time. Hence, this was a trial before the inception of DNA evidence and a person's identification of another was major stuff and sometimes all the evidence that was needed to convict. As Patel and I were leaving the courtroom, I saw an elderly man of at least seventy to eighty years old waiting in the hallway. Based on his age, I knew he had lived through the Jim Crow and the Civil Rights era.

In the past, I, like most oppressed people mistakenly made the assumption that all white folks of that era were not a friend to black folks. The elderly man called to me. He introduced himself as Mr. Rathbone, Donald's father. He wanted to shake my hand. Mr. Rathbone told me that he had no hard feelings toward me. He knew that I was just doing my job. To say I was humbled by his words is to say, again, I was ashamed of myself. Mr. Rathbone knew in his wisdom that I had made the trial in to a personal thing and he forgave me. As much as I thanked him, I needed his forgiveness.

Soon thereafter, Patel quit working for me and went to work for the United States State Department. In Patel's honest and sincere way he asked me, how can you do this shit every day? I had no answer to give him. So, I just wished him luck in his new life and we shook hands. I never heard from or saw Patel again. As for my old basketball coach, I was striking a jury in another murder case. A man I had never met before had the same last name as my former coach. When I inquired, he told me that the coach was his younger brother. I excused him from my jury. I told the prospective juror that I never called his brother coach and to tell his brother that I was fine.

Sentence: *Life plus 10 years*

NIGGAS IN THE VALLEY

Nothing... is more dangerous than sincere ignorance and
conscientious stup dity...Martin I uther King Jr.

I don't know where the idea came from but in the beginning it
seemed to work. The ease of saying that a nigga did it was
all that was needed. Afterwards, in Georgia, you could just as
easily blame it on a Jew and the masses would react the same way,
Leo Frank. Today, it's quite interesting to me, the split between
Jews and black folks seemed to have become nil if not dissipated
over time. Today, only those that are old enough to remember can
recall how it was. We shared in a sense, a similar history, they had
Hitler and we had Mister Charlie.

Both Jews and Blacks alike had second-class citizenship status in
America and they knew it. Some could even argue that the Jews took
Booker T. Washington ideas and merged it W.E.B. Dubois philosophy
for black folks and ran with it. Thus, they have positioned themselves
over generations and prospered as opposed to black folks that became
more systemized and dependent. To the contrary, I know that the
Jewish people had their owned philosophers and beliefs. Thus, they
didn't need advice from black folks to become successful.

Grant reminded me of the same poor white trash that I grew up
with in the Midwest. They lived on the outskirts of my immediate
neighborhood even though we shared the same zip code. As far as I

can remember, the poor white trash were transplants from Kentucky and Tennessee. They came with such a base opinion about Blacks and Jews that defied imagination. I remember little Michael being referred to as poor white trash. Michael had seven brothers and five sisters and his whole family was considered white trash. I recall how Michael could barely read but he had more confidence than everybody.

Michael's family was just as poor if not poorer than anybody in the neighborhood. Still, Michael would call a black person a nigga or a Jew, a kike, as if he was calling your name. Michael had no fear as he racially abused anybody in listening distance. Back then, everybody knew little Michael was just dirt poor and jealous. We were just as poor but no one took Michael seriously. Instead, we had the sincere temerity to look down on Michael and his family as the poor white trash they were.

However, if Michael or his brothers caught a black person or Jew in their neighborhood, they would scream at the top of their lungs, "Niggas in the Valley." When you heard this alarm, you ran for your life and that of your unborn children. Michael and his poor white trash neighbors were filled with so much hate; they'd rather kill you than to know that you were cool.

This imaginary boundary, this corner in the middle of the poorest area in the city of Indianapolis was theirs and they would kill for it. They were so bold. They would jump into their cars and attempt to run you down. Unlike the KKK, they didn't cover their faces. When you would see him in school the next day, you'd say hey Mike what's up, I thought we were cool. Michael would say we are cool, just keep your ass out the valley. I did for the most part.

I remember being chased home from school by poor white trash, as they played chicken with my life. On one occasion, I had to explain to my band teacher how I damaged my baritone as I dropped it to flee. I explained that they chased me home again and attempted to mow me over in a raggedy Chevy with missing hub caps. He understood. Thereafter, I was not allowed to take my instrument home. I remember being forced to walk three miles home from Garfield Park using the railroad tracks to avoid being caught in the valley. At twelve, I had to make this track nearly every day after football practice. It seemed that the poor white trash would give us a pass, when we used the tracks as opposed to the street.

The Jews owned all the stores in the neighborhood and would extend credit to mostly everyone. Back then, your word really meant something and your excuses did too. Pride was a characteristic that mattered to the southern blacks that lived in my neighborhood. As much, if they needed the credit, which most did, being southern they knew not to play with Mr. Charlie's money. So, unlike today, they paid their bills on time.

We had Mr. Passo's that owned the drug store. In the same block Max Shapiro's owned a restaurant and my uncle Ed owned the other restaurant and bar. Mr. Safrine's owned the department store for your back to school savings and Mr. Vogel's and his wife owned the grocery store. I can't recall the name of the Jewish guy that owned the hardware store. However, there was Reagan's Rye next to Shapiro's, the Jewish bakery that would wake up in the Indianapolis winters with the smell of freshly baked bread, rolls and bagels. Reagan's had the best doughnuts in town.

I recall that each one of the Jewish merchants was good to my family and I. A wanting kid will remember who gave him a jet ice cream bar on a hot summer's day or an apple just because you stared at it, for the rest of his life. My parents and community forbade me to beg from not just the Jews but from anybody. Begging was an embarrassment to the family and grounds for a beating. We're set to have my annual fortieth something community reunion real soon.

Grant was an only child and I knew more about who he was and his mentality than he'd ever know about me. People often times perceive me as the middle class super nigga that grew up with a silver spoon in his mouth. To the contrary, they may view me as the poor kid from humble beginnings that made good. However, when you get comfortable in a place, you really don't give a fuck what people think about you and when I met Grant, I was there.

The prosecutor referred to Grant as a skinhead; a troublemaker with a quick temper that liked to point loaded guns at folks. Grant reminded me of the brown haired Italian in the Dirty Dozen that would point his gun and threaten to shoot if he felt slighted in anyway. But, Grant sported naturally blond hair and he was poor white trash or as they say here in the south, a Georgia Cracker. Grant shot his friend in the face as they argued over the caliber and capabilities of a certain gun. Grant knew he had fucked up, so he ran and told his common law wife what he had done. He then convinced her to go along with the age-old story; some Niggas did it. Grant told police essentially that there were some blacks or Mexicans in the valley that he didn't know. After a brief conversation, they attempted to rob him and killed his friend.

Police were all set to believe Grant's story. The detective may have been a Georgia Cracker and inclined to give credibility to such stories as soon as they are made. Besides, police had no reason not to believe Grant. The interviewing detective even left the interview as Grant continued to give his statement to a Caucasian police secretary that looked at Grant with the left eye, as he gave a statement full of inconsistencies.

Sensing the secretary's disbelief, Grant then confessed to her, "Fuck it, I shot him by mistake." The secretary ran for the interviewing cop and told him of the confession. When the cop returned, Grant said that he thought that he needed a lawyer. The cop continued to question Grant about the shooting when Grant again stated that he shot his friend by accident.

Grant's mother was a sweet lady. In meeting her, I figured that she had lost control over Grant many years ago. I also knew that he was not reared the way he was acting in the streets. Grant's mom would remind you of a skinny Aunt Bee of "The Andy Taylor Show." It's been over 10 years since Grant's case was over, but I still think about his mom.

The veteran African American prosecutor that handled Grant's case wanted Grant to pay for all of the tragedies that had befallen black folks for, "it was the Nigga that did it," accusation that led to ones inevitable lynching. I didn't know him personally but rumor had it that he was an enigmatic figure himself. His career was essentially black balled after he prosecuted a black local legend, the Senator for tax evasion. The Senator's wife was battling cancer before she died and the Senator slipped on his taxes. The prosecutor won a conviction, but lost a career in the process. President Carter pardoned his friend and the Senator went on to orchestrate the return of Muhammad Ali into the ring in Georgia after his military draft controversy.

The prosecutor would look at me like how could I represent a skinhead. How could I represent someone that I knew hated me? At one time, I told the prosecutor that Grant was not a skinhead. He asked how I knew, I told him I had met his momma and he wasn't raised that way.

At trial, I tried to keep Grant's statement to police out. I didn't want the jury to hear anything about a confession. The judge allowed Grant's statement to be heard by the jury because he didn't ask for a lawyer he merely said he thought that he needed one. Secondly, I tried to keep his statement he made to his common law wife out. I told the judge that they were married and the statement was privileged between man and wife. The argument died, when wife denied that she was his wife, but merely in an on again off again relationship with Grant. Thus, Grant had to save himself.

The prosecutor called several witnesses and most of them were black. They explained to the jury how Grant walked around the valley and pointed guns at them without reason. How his use of the "N" word was easy for him to say with the automatic weapons he kept on his person at all times. When I went to cross-examine the witnesses, they looked at me as if I were an Uncle Tom, a sell-out. I did my job and as always, I played to win.

The jury convicted Grant of Felony Murder. His mother cried her heart out. She knew that she couldn't do anything to help Grant. She knew that I was about the only person in the room besides her that gave a damn. His common law wife had showed up at the trial with her new beau. I wondered why she came at all. I'll never forget how through her tears, Grant's mother held my face with both her hands and looked me in the eyes, kissed my cheek and quietly said thank you. I told the prosecutor, see, Grant can't be a skinhead.

Sentence: *Life*

YELLOW BITCH SYNDROME

I 've always known that women had some control over me since I've always been a sucker for a beautiful woman. However, I get some comfort in my misery knowing that it's not just me. Men as a class have always done stupid shit to be with the one they want. To the contrary, men who have shown some restraint usually are the ones with the nastiest habits, short of being sexually frustrated if not impotent in my opinion.

The history of men and the bible are rife with examples of how women have changed the course of both. Sampson knew that he was being set up for something bad, but he had to have Delilah anyway. Some theologians just say after she put her head in his lap Sampson was done. There is no report that he actually had her any other way. Cleopatra brought down a nation with her stuff. She was able to turn a son against the man that loved him as a father. Cesar was dead. The masses cried for both Sampson and Cesar. However, the world kept moving to another place. A place where time recorded both instances for what they were, moments in history.

Dena's mother, Sandy sat in my office and explained to me through her tears how she tried to give Dena the life she wanted for herself. I listened patiently, but I could have told her that Dena could never be like her and she could never imagine in her wildest dreams the life of Dena. You could tell that Sandy was fine in her day. In fact, you could see where Dena got her hour glass shape. Dena's smile was not as mastered as Sandy's. Still, Dena's smile was pleasantly controlled. I knew Sandy's smile had different meanings depending on the occasions. Today's occasion was she needed me to save her baby from a life in prison.

As I assessed Dena's mother, Sandy, I wondered if her smile, yellow skin and fine body was all she needed when she was Dena's age. If Sandy's yellow skin had bode well for her in her life? I knew she owned her own hair salon and ever since Dena was born, she's lived in one suburb or another. Sandy told me that the schools systems were very important to her. Dena had the best Sandy could give her. So, how in the world did Dena end up in this mess?

I looked at Dena as if I was looking through her attempting to discern her fascination with wanting to be a nigga or nigga like. Wondering, why or what was so uncool about being a lady. Dena was articulate, smart, pretty and was fine. It didn't take me long to see that Dena was just a pretty yellow bitch that knew she could get a man to do anything. Dena had the "it" factor that made her a fantasy to most men because she was born as she was.

Dena was barely twenty no more than twenty-one, purple accents in her hair; she was a size 4 or 6, about 125 or 130 pounds, with a flat stomach. Petit at 5'4", round apple bottom ass, small waist, a 36 C with full breast, Dena was a fantasy. Looking like a movie star, Dena was just like her momma used to be. The only difference was unlike Dena, Sandy had class and respected her station in life.

Dena's boyfriend Brent was an average young man that talked more shit than he could back up. He was thin with a medium brown complexion. Brent sported a short fade haircut. He stood about 5'8" tall and weighed only a buck-sixty at most. Brent manipulated those around him because they knew of his cousin Dre. Dre was a real thug and had been fighting Brent's battles all of his life. Without Dre, Brent was just another small dude that talked a lot of shit After Dena hooked up with Brent, it didn't take her long to know that he was a chump, a wanna be thug, but there was something about him that she loved.

I asked Sandy to step outside my conference room so that I could speak to Dena alone. Reluctantly, she left. Before I interviewed Dena I asked her a bunch of bullshit questions to build some sort of rapport with her. As if she was seperating the black dirt from the sand, she sat there and carefully answered my questions. At the same time, Dena attempted to control where the conversation would lead. She told me that she worked at a downtown hotel. As I noticed her nails were neat and decorated with all that ghetto shit on them.

I asked Dena if she was hustling at the hotel. Initially, she said no. I asked her how she knew what I was talking about. She said she didn't. She guessed. I knew she was lying to me. So, I asked her again was she selling pussy. I told her that her mother wouldn't have to know. However, if it came out, it was better that I knew now than later. She said sometimes, but she's picky and usually serviced regulars. I knew that was lie number two. I was okay with her showing a little vanity when it came to her stuff.

Dena was a yellow bitch that got men to buy her material things Brent couldn't afford. She knew that she had Brent in a place where he would do anything for her if she pressed him hard enough. I knew what Brent was going through. Most adults will find themselves in an impossible relationship dealing with another that can't be pleased. Seemingly, no matter what you do you can't please them. I've been in that place before with women that happened to be yellow bitches. Unfortunately, I've also been in that place before with judges. They just didn't like me or my client and I got the carry over bullshit they threw at him.

It didn't take long for me to see the real Dena, the spoiled suburban girl trying to live the life of a thug bitch using her complexion as access to men she could use. She asked me, how I knew she was tricking? I told her she looked like she was. Surprised, she didn't know that she looked like a prostitute. Actually, Dena's girlfriend Desire told me they were both tricking when they needed extra money. I had interviewed Desire before Dena got out of jail on bond.

After I directed the meeting with Dena to a more conversational tone, she began to open up and talk more freely. Dena talked so damn much, as she explained what she did and didn't do. At some point, I grew tired of her sanctimonious explanations of why the victim was killed in front her of apartment. Her whining and displaced blame on others was common coming from one that knows that they've fucked up. "Excuses are tools of incompetence used to build monuments of nothing." My law partner Odis would riddle this quote to me when he was frustrated with a nonpaying client.

Dena told me that her neighbor April falsely accused her of stealing some clothes from another neighbor. When she confronted April, her boyfriend jumped in and threatened to beat Brent and Dena's ass. Dena returned to her apartment and tried to convince Brent to confront April's boyfriend. Brent knowing how Dena is known for running her mouth did nothing.

Allegedly, this resulted in Dena talking shit to Brent for hours about how weak he was and how he was a little bitch and scary. Dena compared Brent to April's boyfriend that intervened on her behalf. Dena accused Brent of being cool with this guy disrespecting her. She would then leave her apartment to talk shit to April. Thereafter, return and emasculate Brent.

Dena went on and on fussing and talking shit in the apartment complex about what she would do to April. Declaring in many ways how April wasn't shit. Again, April's boyfriend would intervene. After each confrontation, an infuriated Dena would return to her apartment and complain. This time, however, police claimed that she convinced Brent that April's beau was calling for back up to come and "fuck them up." So, Brent called his cousin Dre.

Dre was in his early twenties, 6 ft tall and was just an angry black man. He was used to fighting for his cousin Brent as they were raised as brothers. Dre brought his posse of five over to Dena's apartment complex and they were all carrying guns. When they arrived, April and her beau locked themselves in their apartment and warned Dre that there were babies inside and they had called the police.

Poonie another neighbor that had nothing to do with the beef between April and Dena began to say shit around Dre and his posse. Anthony another neighbor begged Ponnie to come inside and stop playing with Dre and his crew. Anthony reasoned that Dre didn't know Poonie and secondly, Dre certainly didn't know that Poonie was just a teenaged jokester talking shit. Suddenly, someone from Dre's crew shot and killed Ponnie on the spot since they had come over to shoot someone anyway. Dre fled with his posse. Poonie was only seventeen years old.

When police arrived for April's 911 call, they were now investigating a homicide. After a brief investigation, Brent and Dena were arrested and charged with murder. Dena's mouth in a left-handed sort of way was just as responsible as Poonie's stupid ass for his murder, so police thought. And, Brent's silly ass, he just fell victim to the yellow bitch syndrome.

The yellow bitch syndrome is just like any other syndrome. It's a pathology that can be innate or environmental. Syndrome comes from the Greek expression meaning a collection of things that run together: a cause and effect scenario. Yellow bitches that suffer from this syndrome have an expectation of people, places and things that others do not have. This expectation is based on their idea of beauty, yellow skin and long pretty hair (LPH), which gives them an entitlement superior to others. The yellow bitch syndrome is a condition that equally applies to men.

The attitudes of those affected by the yellow bitch syndrome are capsulated in arrogance and vanity comparable to the pathology of narcissism. The ripple effect of this attitude is the foundation for the delusion expectation of entitlement. Unlike most, who are taught the lie that if you just work hard you can obtain the things you need to be happy. Thus, having lower expectations is not always a bad thing. The more you want runs parallel with the higher anxiety or frustration when it's not obtainable. If you're not careful, with a straight face, the yellow bitch will try to convince you that it's okay to continue to take care of her even when she's found a new man. Simply because you said that you would, when you thought she was yours.

Don't get me wrong. I believe that behind every good man is a good woman. I believe that a man that finds a wife finds a good thing. To the contrary, someone inflicted with the yellow bitch syndrome believes she supersedes her role as a wife and becomes that of trophy. Likewise, she's only to be taken out and displayed. From time to time, she's to be polished up to stay shiny and new. Thus, the role of wife is in name only. She believes she's more of a partner. I believe, for one, that you can't be both. At least, not with me, when I'm paying for everything.

However, as with every one, Father Time and Mother Nature will pay those a visit that suffer from yellow bitch syndrome. When this happens, their vanity will give in to gravity and they will be introduced to their mortality. But, rest assured, those that possess the syndrome will pass this pathology down to their children. Thus, here I sit with Dena with her yellow tattooed skin, ghetto nails and purple accented hair.

Strangely, a man would sell his soul to the devil to be with her. For many, the yellow bitch becomes the cross roads before a brother begins to date white women. For white men, the yellow bitch ain't too black, which makes her just black enough to desire her stuff. White men will convince her that she has an exotic look about herself. He will shower her with praise and gifts before he consumes her as if she's a bowl of cereal. The yellow bitch syndrome is as old as America herself. Sadly, even today, some yellow bitches won't tell you, but they know that they've benefited from the syndrome because someone simply thought them pretty.

The yellow bitch has had so many fools to come her way. She begins to believe that her yellow skin and her long pretty hair (LPH) gives her license to use a fool that allows himself to be used. Before long, she too becomes lost in her moral responsibility to teach a man to be a man. She begins to enjoy the perks that come along with her yellow skin. If one thought real hard about the yellow bitch, one could come to put all of them in the same basket and despise them all. But, I'm reminded that the yellow bitch syndrome was not created by her, but by men. Thus, like the rest of us, they should be treated, as you would like to be treated. To the contrary, how crazy is the pathology of those that had to have one, as Oprah was to Steadman; I was to June and Brent was to Dena.

As I sat there with Dena, the alleged proof was in the pudding. Brent called Dre to do violence to April's boyfriend but Poonie was killed instead. All of this occurred because Dena, a descendant of the yellow bitch syndrome passed down to her from her mother; felt that someone had to die for calling her out over some stolen clothes. Dena knew that Brent would have done anything for her. Brent was in love.

Funny how, Brent had no idea of how much of her stuff Dena had sold when she worked at the hotel. If Brent had known, he probably would have called Dre anyway. As a society, we can't count all the people that have been killed in the name of love. I understood Brent's commitment to love, however misplaced it was.

Like me, Brent didn't understand that some people have drifted too far away and have become too emotionally crippled to be capable of giving love. Likewise, they can only accept love with strings ominously attached. Those of us who recognize this emotional imbalance know that we're dealing with a yellow bitch or one that has drowned in the quicksand of delusion, selfishness and conceit. Still, like a coward we learn to love them in-spite of themselves because of our fear of being alone or the misassumption that we have someone special.

When the case was called to trial, Prescott Richards and I had the charges dismissed against Dena and Brent, we argued that even assuming Brent called his cousin Dre, his act of shooting Poonie was a separate crime. Thus, it would be a different story if April or her beau had been shot or Poonie was shot as Dre's crew tried to shoot April. No, Poonie was shot because he went around them gangster ass thugs talking shit.

After Dena's case was dismissed, Prescott and I ran into Walter Robinson as we were leaving the courthouse and like always, we decided to go get something to eat. I don't know where we ended up, but Prescott and I began to discuss as men do the merits of my yellow bitch syndrome observations. Walter was surprisingly quiet, as Prescott discussed the flaws of my argument. Prescott correctly discerned that my observations could apply to any woman or man. However, Prescott and I agreed that Dena and her mother were beautiful women and were fine as hell.

I asked Walter if he agreed. Being the innate contrarian he is, it didn't matter if we had described Dena as a Halle Berry look-a-like. Walter's response would have been the same. Walter replied, "Are ya'll talking about that slew footed girl that spoke with a lisp that was walking behind ya'll?" Prescott and I replied, yes. Walter then asked, "With the thick yellow woman wearing the clothes that were too tight?" Prescott and I replied, yes. Walter exacting in on the subject asked, "The one behind ya'll with the swollen ankles and ankle meat coming over her shoes?" Huh? Walter replied, "Them bitches were just all right." "Put ya'll jack back in the box!"

Dena's mother sent me a letter thanking me and informing me that she was not going to pay the balance of my attorney fees. She told me that my services were no longer needed. I guess not. However, I found her attitude consistent with the behavior of entitlement I had observed all- along. The attitude of wanting something for nothing, she felt that she didn't have to pay the rest of my fees knowing that it was my skill that had Dena's murder case dismissed.

However flawed my logic was, I could have sued her in an attempt to break the syndrome and collected on the fifteen-thousand she owed me. But, I didn't. So, I just chalked it up to the game. In fact, I was silly to have expected anything more because I knew that I was dealing with a yellow bitch. Thus, I should have expected her behavior to be as it was, one of entitlement.

I SAT NEXT TO THE DEVIL

T oday I sat next to the Devil. I was afraid but at the same time I was curious. I wanted to see how he would communicate with me. I wanted to check out his reasoning skills. Was his attitude one of discernment? Was his disposition calm or was it one of rage? At first, I had no real expectation other than my fear of the unknown. As he sat in the cage inside the jail, he looked remarkably normal to me. I had seen ancient paintings of his likeness in one-way or the other. Typically it would be a man dressed in red and black with pointed ears. Some say that he favored a werewolf but in the 1970's he resembled a child.

I introduced myself as his lawyer. It was ironic that I would be chosen to represent the Devil, although I could have declined the appointment. I admit that I was curious to see if I could challenge my oath to represent all that were in need of exerting what ever constitutional rights they were entitled to. The reality of it all was that I wanted to represent him and in that also self-evaluate. This need for me to self-evaluate was imminent. I don't know why. At that moment, something was pressing the need, something drawing me in. Although I tried to remain objective about my purpose, I was intrigued and consumed with sitting next to a person that had taken life for the sake of just taking.

As we discussed his personal information, he often times held his head slightly titled forward. His eyes seemed to position themselves as if he were looking up at me even though we were both seated. For a black man, he did have a pointed nose like I had seen in an ancient drawing of the Devil. He had a full set of teeth that were unremarkable. His incisors were no sharper or pointed as the next person. His hair was cut short about a half inch all the way around with a premature receding hairline. The Devil stood about 5'10, 175lbs to 185lbs. He was very dark but not to the extent that his complexion made him remarkable or different from others that were as dark or darker.

The Devil sounded rather illiterate but he was not. His voice was coarse and unemotional. I got the impression that he was trying to be rather nice to me. Although, this didn't impress me, I remained cordial and as nonjudgmental as one could sitting next to the Devil.

As we continued to go over his basic information of where he lived and worked. There came a time as with most conversations, where we connected. At that point, he knew that I knew that he was the Devil. It wasn't anything he said or did; it was just one of those spiritual moments where the ethos or essence of him showed itself clear. Of course, I was paying attention to everything he said and his body language.

Yes, I was on guard and curiously anxious for something anything to happen. But, instead, it was just a spirit. His spirit had entered the room and remained as I questioned him about his educational background. I asked the Devil if he had even finished high school. I asked the Devil if he could read.

His subterfuge was subtle almost passive. But, I kept or attempted to keep my guard up without coming off as frightened. I don't know why I was so preoccupied with allowing the Devil to know that I wasn't afraid of him. I know and would expect that most people would be petrified merely being in his presence. But, me, I wanted him to know that I wasn't. Of course I was sitting on one side of the room made of metal and brick and he was on the other side of the bulletproof glass.

As the Devil began to profess his innocence to me, I sat there patiently and listened to his stories of murder. In a moment of reflection, I thought that when you think of the Devil, you think of one that has all power second only to God. You don't think that the Devil can be contained by cement, metal and glass. I expected him to have some super powers that transcended imagination of what a mere mortal like me could conceive. Thereafter, I learned that my idea of who I thought he was gave him power or influence over me that he had not earned.

As I sat with the Devil, he reminded me of my friends from other countries. They too try to assimilate into western culture. Some of my African friends are more patriotic and westernized than I could ever be. One Ethiopian friend told me that he would tell me where to go if I were to visit his country, but he's not interested in going with me. Today, he's serving twenty years in federal prison for drug trafficking. It's amazing to me that once he got out of jail on bond, he didn't choose to flee to Africa and get loss.

As the Devil continued to show me his efforts of assimilation, I remained cautious of him. It's human nature for someone as liberal as me to attempt to humanize everyone, but how does one begin to humanize the Devil. I don't know if anyone but the naive can. So as naive person I at least tried. I allowed my humanity to get in the way and I treated the Devil with civility. After much effort, I couldn't humanize the Devil. However, I could identify with the isolation of how it feels to be unwanted.

The more he talked of his innocence the less enchanted I became with him. The more he explained himself the less innocuous his powers became. Thus, the more he said, the less impressive he became until he became next to nothing. His frantic conversation of innocence was reduced to a spirit. Certainly, a spirit that did not have a life of it's own but one that needed another's to survive. A spirit that needed for me to believe in it so that he could breathe. The Devil's spirit was not self-sustaining. Imagine that the Devil needed you or me in order to survive.

Mr. Hardy was in his mid to late fifties. He lived outside of Detroit and had worked over twenty years in a car factory before the Devil killed him. Mr. Hardy was a religious and solid family man that was married over thirty years. He was passing through Atlanta going to Florida to take his expectant daughter some new baby furniture. Excited about the baby, Mr. Hardy had worked that day before he began his journey to Florida. Finding himself exhausted, he stopped at a well-known national hotel that was located in the ghetto. The hotel known for its economy prices and right off the highway would be Mr. Hardy's last stop.

Mr. Hardy pulled into the hotel. As he checked in, the Devil sat there patiently and watched Mr. Hardy exit the lobby and return to his truck. As Mr. Hardy parked in front of his room, he unlocked the door to his room, left the door opened and returned to his truck for his luggage. As Mr. Hardy returned to the truck, like the night, the Devil slipped inside of his room and waited for his return. As Mr. Hardy returned to his room and closed the door, the Devil ambushed him.

Mr. Hardy refused to be intimidated and began to fight for his life and that's exactly what he gave. A shot to the face right through his wired rim glasses is all it took. The Devil had killed Mr. Hardy with the precision of a marksman. I still see photos of Mr. Hardy as he's laying flat on his back on top his bed facing the ceiling with his coat still on. As I prepared for trial, I'd wish that Mr. Hardy would have just given him the money. I suppose that would not have been enough for the Devil, as he's in to the collection of souls. Instead, the State in opening statements shared facts about the grandfather that was murdered bringing his grandbaby something to sleep on. Mr. Hardy's daughter was nine months pregnant at the time of his death.

Later in life, I hope that child's mother will simply tell her that your Granddaddy died because he loved you so much. I hope she's told of how much of a man he was and served as an example to others. As she gets older, I hope she's told that her Grandfather was killed for no other reason than the spirit of evil and opportunity left him vulnerable, but his death darling had nothing to do with you.

The only witness to Mr. Hardy's murder was a crack head prostitute that observed the Devil slip into his hotel room. However, the prostitute died of Aids before trial. Also, there was a man that the Devil wanted to share the blame with, a partner in crime that had refused the Devil's invitation to hit a lick at the hotel. I'm used to beating up on partners in crime. I thought that I could do enough to discredit him. Who would believe a man that the Devil felt comfortable enough to share a crime? Moreover, the murder weapon had never been found. Even if I'm just counting the time myself for a minute, the Devil had a chance at acquittal.

Miguel was in his early twenties when he met the Devil. Known as a very hard worker who enjoyed the fruits of his labor, Miguel was like any other Mexican in that on Fridays, he'd drink as much beer as he could and on Saturday mornings he'd play soccer with his friends. This was after a long week of hard laborious work on a job that most Americans didn't want for the money or lack thereof. I always thought it was a noble thing to leave every one you know to come to America and shovel her shit. Only to send part of every check home so others could eat. Sadly, some people and cultures will live off of you for as long as they can. Soon, your charity becomes an expectation that filters into a demand tied into some emotional shit that has nothing to do with the charity you extended in the first place.

One Friday, Miguel was drunk and asleep in his moderately new pickup truck. The Devil found Miguel and attempted to rob him, when Miguel resisted, a shot to the face. Miguel was dead. The same gun that killed Mr. Hardy was now used to kill Miguel. The police surmised as much since it was the same bullets removed from each body. I had hoped that Miguel had sent the money home to his family before he was killed.

The Devil intentionally sought out victims in Miguel's highly populated illegal immigrant community. He knew that immigrants don't like calling the police. As much as they hate to use banks to transact their business, they work here and wire money back to Mexico. It's not surprising that Mexicans don't trust Americans. Americans relentlessly reminds them at every chance she gets, it's you that has my life so fucked up. But, hey, it wouldn't be America if she didn't have someone to fuck over. The Devil knew that the Mexican immigrants were a vulnerable people only here seeking a better life and willing to work for it in the shadows. The Devil is all about opportunity for mayhem, misfortune and death.

I wondered when did killing become so easy for the Devil. I guess some would think that's a stupid question, but it isn't considering that the Devil started out as one of God's favorite angels. I never understood the mindset that one life has more value than the other. However, society has convinced herself of this conceit. Certainly, the death of a family member is always more painful than that of a stranger. To the contrary, the death of an illegal immigrant is much like the death of a street nigga, next case. Sadly, Miguel had no family here to identify his body. Another immigrant worker was given the honor of telling authorities who he was.

Police arrested the Devil as he solicited an undercover cop for sex. The Devil was cruising in midtown, Atlanta's largely gay community looking for an unsuspecting lonely soul. There was no doubt in my mind that the Devil was about to rob and kill the cop he thought was a weak fag. To the Devil, he viewed the fag as another member of a vulnerable group he could take advantage of or trick.

After a two-week trial, the Devil was convicted by a jury of his peers. The partner in crime the Devil had offered to work with told the jurors that the Devil had bragged about both murders. A crack head surfaced and told the jury that the Devil gave him a gun to sell that was the same caliber as the murder weapon. Moreover, the Devil had made a documentary home video holding the same caliber gun used to kill both victims. As much as I huffed and puffed during the trial, the jury believed the state's witnesses. So, did I. Nonetheless, I wondered if the jury knew that they were in the presence of the Devil. I wondered if they thought that they were just in the presence of another man.

People have asked me, why was I so eager to represent the Devil, why was my need to self evaluate to this extreme relevant? I know that I have posed similar questions to those few that have climbed Mount Everest or bungee jumped from a bridge. What was the thrill? Was it the act itself or the bragging rights that comes with the perceived triumph of standing on top of the mountain or dangling from the end of a rubber cord suspended upside down? Why was the conduct or need to conquer necessary?

For me, I simply confronted a spiritual fear whether actual or imaginary. If I'm better for it, which I feel that I am, then that's a good thing right? So be it, my humanity was challenged and it stood tall. Yes, I'm better for it much like the man that successfully climbed the mountain. To the contrary, the mountain will never see or judge those that will attempt to conquer her. However, I know how it feels to be viewed upon as a Devil when some folks look at me. Having sat next to a Devil, I know that there's more than one and I am not he.

Sentence: *Consecutive life.*

CHAPTER TWO

OEDIPUS

COMPUTER LOVE

W hen he emerged from the bushes, the officers stopped and questioned him. The officers asked him what he was doing in the bushes. Bruce replied rather smugly," I was taking a piss." The officers asked for his credentials before they ran a check on the car. As they conversed with Bruce, the dispatcher announced that the car was clean. Thus, it had not been reported as stolen. After they recorded Bruce's identifiers onto a note book pad, they released him. As Bruce jumped into that 300 series BMW, the officers quipped, "Hey Johnny, if we were to go into the bushes we wouldn't find a dead body?" When Bruce quipped back," I don't think so." They all laughed at the notion of a body being found in the bushes as they drove away. It would take weeks before Sheila's body would be found.

Knowing what I know now, I wondered if Bruce was just so confident in his abilities to lie with a straight face and sell the lie as if he were selling a used car. Bruce was confident in his belief that he had hidden Sheila's body so well in the brush and bushes near the busiest airport in the world. He actually thought that he wouldn't get caught. Amazingly, the police allowed Bruce to just hop in his car and just leave. Any other time, police would have stopped an African American in his tracks just for driving such a car. That whole police profiling thing does exist.

Perhaps, however, Bruce knew exactly what macho shit to say to the macho police. You know, that whole Jeffery Dalmer thing, when police saw the Asian boy running down the street high out of his head with Dalmer pursuing him. After Dalmer explained that they were lovers, Milwaukee's finest just turned the guy back over to Dalmer. Dalmer literally had the Asian boy for dinner with a white wine.

Unbeknownst to the officers, Bruce had presented them with fake identification. The night before, Bruce had robbed a city worker Johnny Rogers of his wallet and identification. Johnny had got so intoxicated at the club that Bruce followed him home and robbed him. Bruce found the Johnny passed out in his car in front of his Mother's house. Johnny in his drunken state attempted to fight Bruce over his wallet. But, he was no match for the sober ex-Marine.

Bruce had been dishonorably discharged from the Marines for theft and other unrelated charges and had served time in Leavenworth Federal Prison. Bruce was the oldest of three kids to a mother who was less than twenty years his senior. She had her last two with another man. Bruce's, mother and sister worked in Corporate America. There came a time when Bruce became an embarrassment to his mom.

Bruce knew his little brother looked up to him in spite of how their mother treated him. Bruce always knew his little brother was her favorite. His brother's father was just as proud to have a son. But, unlike them, his little brother would have followed Bruce to his grave. To the contrary, it didn't turn out that way. Destiny and life carried the day or as we say in the south, God took over and Bruce's younger brother was killed. Bruce's mother blamed Bruce for his death. It was never clear to me if Bruce was somehow involved or responsible for his younger brother's death. However, it was clear to me that Bruce blamed himself for it. Regretfully, it may have been the things his grieving mother said to him as they laid his little brother to rest that triggered Bruce's downward spiral.

I know words can hurt. Especially, hurtful words from those you love and respect. In fact, words can damage a life. If those hurtful words come from a parent, you can measure a child's confidence and success or lack thereof. My childhood friend was a victim of words. His mother would call him names in front of his friends and I. She would trivialize his feeling and dreams until she had taken the hope out of him. Today, my friend is fifty years old and has never accomplished anything in his life. He gets started but never finishes. He's learned to mask his lack of confidence with drugs, women and music. However, get him fired up with the least bit of perceived disrespect from a woman and he becomes criminally violent to her.

"Tall dark and handsome; a workout buff; Ex-Marine; love mystery movies and jazz; considers himself a hopeless romantic." When I read Bruce's computer profile on Negro planet.com, I knew he was full of shit. I knew he had used all of the code words that would give one the sense that he was a heavy thinker. Bruce brooding in the dark back corner of the jazz club Church Hill Grounds breaking down the lyrical phrases of Coltrane. To the contrary, Bruce was just not that deep. However, he didn't need to be once viewers saw the shirtless Ex-Marine profile picture.

Computer dating was new when Bruce began to use it as a tool to meet unsuspecting lonely and trusting women. Bruce knew from the onset that he was a predator looking for a desperate woman in need of love if not guidance. Bruce was a predator looking for an opportunity. I guess that observation may apply to many whom try to find companionship online.

However, the ringer with online dating is you never know if you're connecting with that true or sincere companion that's absent in your life. You never know if you're conversing with another Bruce who didn't give a damn about the world after his brother was killed. Especially, a woman trapped in low self esteem and loneliness. I know from personal experience how lonely; lonely can be. How dreadful the silence can compromise an otherwise simple existence into something that it is not, complicated.

"Pleasantly plump, love to laugh. I'm a photographer, who can make any smile look like a million dollars. I love jazz and mystery movies. However, I demand honesty. If you fit the bill, holla back, Sheila." Sheila was beautiful to me. She had a beautiful smile almost girly, like she could not believe she was photographing herself to place in her ad, a profile picture. Shielding her plumpness, she sported a black turtleneck sweater and she had this thick curly hair. Given her complexion, Sheila appeared to be bi-racial.

Bruce and Sheila appeared to hit it off immediately. Being so honest in her profile, Sheila was an easy win for Bruce. However, just like any other honeymoon, the romance was short lived. Sheila was specific in what she wanted in a man inside and out. Like most, Sheila wanted a little better than what would have approached her on the streets. Moreover, she insisted on honesty. So, when she found out that Bruce was a fraud she told her friend that she was about to break it off. By this time, Bruce was walking around thinking the pussy was his and driving Sheila's beamer more than her. Telling himself that he was doing the fat girl a favor in exchange for the life he wanted to live but couldn't afford. After Bruce knew Sheila had caught him in a number of lies, Bruce saw the relationship unfolding. The writing was on the wall, it was over or about to be.

Bruce's sister and I worked out at the same gym. We would exchange pleasantries and kept it moving. I would see her before I even knew of Bruce. It was merely coincidental that we shared the same gym and knew the same people there. At times, she appeared to be very pensive, as if, she thought I would tell her secrets. But, I would never divulge dirty secrets of others. It's my job if not my life. Keeping my mouth shut was something I got from home. When I'd run home and share gossip with my mother, she'd say if she could just mine her own business, she'd be just fine. Thus, you should do the same. Followed by, "did you do those chores I asked you to do the day before? See, if you weren't in to everybody's business you could have finish what I told your ass to do."

Bruce's sister was tall and had an athletic build. She was about 5'10" flat abs and nice legs for a black woman. You could say that she took after her mother because they both had nice round asses. When I did flirt with her, she told me, "I thought that you wanted my Mom?" I acted all surprised by her statement that I flirted with her mother. I was guilty. Therefore, she didn't bite and neither did momma.

With his Marine days long behind him, Bruce still looked like a Marine. 6'2", 180 pounds with less than 10 percent body fat. Bruce had broad shoulders, flat abs and sported a tapered faded haircut. I don't recall much facial hair and he appeared to be very neat for a man. I didn't want to believe that Bruce was as cold as police said he was, but who other than a cold person can strip a woman naked and stuff her panties in her mouth. Duct taped her mouth shut from beneath her eyes to the bottom of her neck. Thereafter, throw her in the bushes as if she were an old tire.

I had studied the crime scene photos of Sheila's butt-naked body, arms bound by duct tape, pussy exposed with one sock on covered by the bushes and the brush. I wondered who the message was for. Bruce stuffed her panties in her mouth for a reason. He had only known Sheila less than thirties days, now she's dead. Messages are left for the living. It could be that Bruce stuffed them in her mouth because she talked too damn much. Like most men, he couldn't take it when she confronted him with his lies.

Whatever Sheila said or didn't say, she didn't deserve this from Bruce. I'm convinced that Bruce was sending the message to another, perhaps to his mother. The one figure in is life whose love he needed but didn't feel that he had. The respect he was never able to garner from her even as a child and then as a Marine. The blame she placed at his feet for his younger brother's death. Was Bruce sending her a message because he could not kill her and too self centered to kill himself?

Sadly, Sheila's body remained missing for a number of weeks. Same old shit, people, family and friends began looking for her after she failed to show up in the places she was supposed to be. Most police departments have a 48 hours rule when a person is gone missing before a report is taken. Atlanta is no different.

A man walking his dog on a trail near the airport found Sheila's naked body. As police reports were filed and circulated throughout the various police agencies, the two cops that had encountered Bruce coming out of those very bushes contacted the lead detective on the case. Thereafter, they provided the lead detective with the fake name and address Bruce had provided. Luckily, at least, they were smart enough to write it down. This information was checked out, which led police to Johnny Rogers, the drunk-ass city worker that had been robbed of his wallet on the same day Bruce had encountered police walking out of the bushes.

Can you imagine the look on the cops' faces when they learned that a body had in fact been dumped in the bushes as they encountered Bruce. As police questioned Sheila's friends, they learned of her computer love, Bruce. At the same time, Sheila's friends told police that Sheila was to meet with Bruce to end their relationship because she had learned that he had lied to her. Sheila's friends told police that Sheila didn't care how fine Bruce was, he lied to her about who he was and it was over. Shortly, thereafter, she was never seen again.

Police went and pulled Bruce's DMV picture and got an address on him. Initially, when they approached Bruce, they wanted to know the last time he had seen Sheila? Police told Bruce that Sheila was dead. Her body had been found near the airport. Bruce asked police, "Why ya'll telling me?" Police replied, "We thought you would care?" Bruce retort was, "I don't." At that point, police knew they had their man.

Police took Bruce's DMV photo and placed it in a photo array and took it to the drunken city worker. He identified Bruce as the person that robbed him of his wallet. Police then canvassed a hotel where Bruce was known to frequent on Fulton Industrial Blvd. Whatever vice you have boys, girls and drugs you can find on Fulton Industrial Blvd, about twenty miles west of Atlanta. There, they found a cleaning lady who identified Bruce, but didn't remember Sheila.

The cleaning lady recalled seeing Bruce as the guy that drove that pretty 300 series BMW just yesterday. The problem was Sheila had now been dead for over three weeks. Sheila's friend told police that Sheila was not the type of person that let people drive her car. Certainly, not the guy she was about to dump. Police now had motive and circumstantial evidence to arrest Bruce and they did.

At trial, the police that encountered Bruce emerging from the bushes testified as did the city worker he had robbed. They explained how Bruce used Johnny Roger's identification with police. The cleaning lady identified Bruce as the person with the white 300 series BMW that she saw at the hotel. Bruce didn't testify. He just sat next to me eerily quiet throughout the whole trial. Bruce acted as if he didn't care about the outcome or as if he wasn't there.

The only two occasions I did see any emotion from Bruce was when I discussed his dead younger brother. The second was time was when the jury found him guilty of Sheila's murder. Each time, a single tear fell from his right eye from which he quickly wiped away not wanting me or anyone to see it.

Sentence: *Life*

HE'S YOUR SON NOT YOUR MAN

When I met Wendell he was only twenty-one or twenty-two years old and the oldest of three children. He had a younger brother and sister still in high school. His mother, Susan was in her late thirties or early forties at best and she had Wendell when she was a teenager. Susan suffered from low self-esteem and was not what I would consider attractive. She was a rather frumpy woman with a brown complexion and had acne scattered about her face. She had trouble making eye contact and appeared rather timid when I met her. Susan even muttered it seemed as she explained herself.

I don't know if there was a history of abuse in all of Susan's relationships but I do know there was a significant history of abuse with her current one. Susan's husband, Henry was roughly the same age as her, medium brown complexion 5'10 well built but not stocky, somewhat muscular. Henry from what I could gather was a bully. His method of doing things was to bully Susan and have her bully the kids for his sake.

Wendell had moved out of the house by the time Susan had married Henry. Wendell lived nearly three miles from Susan with his pregnant girlfriend. Even though Henry was cool with Wendell and treated him with respect. Through his siblings, Wendell would hear horrifying stories of physical and emotional abuse inflicted by Henry toward his mom. Confused, Wendell would try to be cordial with Henry. However, Wendell had a lot of reservations in terms of being too cordial because the stories of abuse were in the back of his mind. In fact, Wendell's siblings told him that they were afraid of Henry and what he might do to them. So, as their older brother, they looked to Wendell for help.

On one occasion, Wendell had words with Henry after Susan decided to call him during an argument. I don't know why Susan called Wendell because she had older brothers that were adult men. One would think that Susan's brothers were much more mature than Wendell to handle a domestic situation. More importantly, Susan could have called police if she felt her life or the life of her kids were in jeopardy.

After that argument, Wendell made it to Susan's house and confronted Henry. The argument became heated as Wendell talked about the abuse and how Henry treated Susan. As the argument escalated, threats were made between the two. Henry threatened Susan that he would deal with Wendell if she didn't. Wendell told Henry that he was going to deal with him if he continued to abuse his mom and siblings. Henry chuckled at Wendell, the man-child standing up for his momma before he threatened Wendell again. "Boy you don't know who you're fucking with."

To the average person, Susan knew or should have known that nothing good could have occurred by calling Wendell to help her resolve her arguments with her husband. She didn't have the right to involve her man-child in her adult affairs. Besides, it was her fucked up marriage not his. Sometime ago, Wendell had owned a small caliber .38 pistol. There was nothing special about the gun other than the fact that it was cheap and could be bought off the streets fairly easily.

Days went by before the next argument occurred. Wendell received a call from his frightened desperate mother with her voice quivering over the phone. In the background, Wendell heard all kinds of obscenities from Henry to the effect of tell that motherfucker to come on over here. I got something for him. From the tone of the call, it was apparent to Wendell that Henry was again beating Susan. Wendell told me that he didn't remember hanging the phone up or even the drive to Susan's place. I told him to just remember that when he walked into Susan's house his gun was in his pocket.

When he entered the house he was confronted by Henry. A struggled ensued, when Wendell unceremoniously pulled out his .38 and shot Henry in the chest area. Henry died in the house before paramedics could arrive. At the request of Susan, Wendell fled. No one knew where Wendell was hiding. Police figured that one of Wendell's uncles put Wendell away on ice at least until they hired me.

Wendell's family was referred to me by a lady that worked within the court system that was friends with one of Wendell's uncles. I don't know the extent of their relationship and never asked. However, I was humbled by the referral because it is something when people trust you with the life of someone they love.

In Georgia, there are three possible outcomes when a person is convicted of murder: One is the death penalty; two is life in prison without the possibility of parole and thirdly, life in prison with parole. I have always enjoyed the sport or challenge of explaining why people kill each other. I've always loved the opportunity to suggest to others that but for the grace of God it could be you sitting to my right. I know that when domestic situations get out of hand anyone is capable of killing another. Most of us are not emotionally strong or compassionate enough to walk away when our hearts are broken.

Wendell was eventually arrested and I requested a hearing to get him out of jail on bond. As much as there are things about the South that you could absolutely hate there are equally a number of things you would love. One of those things is chivalry. In the South, manners like please and thank you are still very important. Moreover, to show and present yourself with manners will avail you to a certain code in the South; a dignity or humanity where you will be treated with civility.

I'm not saying that chivalry only exists in the South, but it may run deeper than anywhere I've been. So in my case, the facts were that a young man running to defend his mother from an abusive husband is something that runs very, very deep. A young man that killed defending the honor of his mother could be construed as an act of chivalry or at least self-defense. Thus, to show that sort of chivalry one could avail oneself to the code.

For generations, white men have placed white women on a pedestal. The white woman has traditionally been revered as some sort of angel that every man thinks that he wants or should want. So to show acts of kindness toward a white woman and then any woman, hopefully the code of chivalry could spill over and cloak you with thoughts of civility. Thus, perhaps you could derive some benefit from the code. Even, when protecting a black woman after she brought home an abusive dick around her kids.

Wendell's case occurred on the Southern part of town about forty miles from Atlanta. For those that are not familiar with Atlanta, black people come hear to chase their dreams. For over a hundred years, Atlanta has been a bastion of success stories and opportunities for black people from W.E.B. Dubois to Martin Luther King Jr; to BabyFace, Ludacris, India Arie, Jermaine Dupri, Spike Lee, Jasmine Guy and the great Ozzie Davis; Atlanta was the place to be. However, once you leave Atlanta you are in Georgia and Georgia has not evolved itself as a state as Atlanta has evolved itself to be an international city.

I attempted to use the fact that we were in Georgia to Wendell's advantage. I began to devise a defense that showed the systematic and random abuse of Susan. I was able to do that even though Susan was not the most articulate woman I had ever met. In preparing Susan for her interviews with homicide detectives, I was sure that they would leave the interview having some empathy for her.

When you hear of abuse, in particular, torture, subconsciously the conversation becomes did the abuse in fact occur? After the abuse is acknowledged, why didn't the abused person leave? More importantly, did the abuser deserve to die because of it? In any given circumstances, some people would say yes, some no and some would be on the fence. They would be on the fence not because they were indifferent to the abuse. They would be on the fence because they just wouldn't know who to trust or what to believe. Given the fact that we were in the Southern suburb of Atlanta, people there would most likely say yes, the abuser deserved to die. They would reason that if a man struck a woman, then the motherfucker had what was coming to him. Hence, that was the part of the South that I was banking on. The part that stilled believed in the code.

I don't know why some women or mothers rear their sons to be their man and savior. One could almost get the impression that women rear their sons to be the man that they want for themselves as opposed to rearing him to be a responsible person. Some would argue that both methods of rearing a boy could co-exist and can be mutually exclusive. To the contrary, I think a young man nurtured in this quasi-love connection with his momma will fail in his relationships with women if not, fail in life. He will fail because he will try to find his mother in his mate. He will fail because he will learn that no woman will treat him like his momma. Selfishly, in her need to remain relevant, momma will refuse to tell him that her brand of love is not out there and it will die with her. Thus, leaving an emotionally handicap son behind searching for a love that doesn't exist.

As momma keeps her breast in his mouth for too long, he will fail to learn how to stand up and piss. By the time he becomes a teenager, his ambition in life is nominal at best and as he gets older, he's okay, much to momma's chagrin, of living his life in her basement. Which begs the question, should a mother rear her son and feed him some of the stuff she wants in a man: can anything good come from it? Is it healthy? Obviously, something bad comes from it, if it's not held in check.

My mother would chastise me when I would attempt to intervene in her arguments with my dad. She would simply tell me to stay out of grown folks business along with a smack in the mouth. My mother never allowed me to cross the line or even give an opinion of the many problems she had with my father. However, I never had to deal with a Henry or boyfriend of my mother. Unlike Wendell's circumstances, I never saw my mother with another man. I never had notions or ideas about killing my father. I only from time to time dreamt about how it would be if we had simply moved away. To spare my mom from the verbal and emotional abuse he would inflict.

As a result of my mother not allowing me to cross the line, to hear my parents argue was synonymous with keep your mouth shut and mind your own business. If it was daylight outside, you were probably better off to just leave the house or hangout in the yard until the argument stopped or dad left.

The Greeks taught us about the Oedipus complex where the young boy fantasies about his mother and that fantasy includes wanting her sexually. I have never thought about my mother sexually but I, like most young boys had an innate instinct to protect my mother against the world including against my own father.

It was funny growing up with five brothers, to have one of us to snap back at my mom only to have the other four to look at you like "who the fuck are you talking to." So, we all felt the same innate instinct to protect mother. Luckily, my father acknowledged this and that was one of the reasons other than age, he and mother didn't argue as much. Dad once told us that there were too many of us to kill referencing to his five sons. At some point in time, my father realized that could be a possibility.

On one occasion I came home from college for the summer. My brother Bill, the crazy one that was the only son still living with my parents snapped back at my father because of his tone with my mother. My father was frustrated with my mother. At the time, mother was going through the early stages of Alzheimer's and no one including my father knew what Alzheimer's was. I thought my father was going to kill Bill right there on the spot by stabbing him in the neck. Bill who loved his fireweed as he does was probably high, when he snapped at my father in mother's defense "You don't have to talk to her that way."

Dad was so shitty that his lips began to tremble and his dentures damn near slipped out of his mouth. My dad's body began to shake from his self-imposed restraint. Never had dad taken such insubordination from any of his kids before but he was older and wiser now. At the time, I thought that I was about to witness a murder or be a part of one or be killed myself, but the one choice I didn't have was to stand around and do nothing.

The fear and tension of that moment was overwhelming. I can't explain, It was that overwhelming. Dad had always taught us if we were going to do something, do it first. Dad knew what he had taught us. We as a family never had been one for conversation before a fight. Throw the first blow and throw so hard that your target will think about if he wants to get back up or if he's ready to die today. In spite of the fear, dad knew that he had taught his boys to kill the noise.

I don't know why dad calmed down, but there was a time when he would have shot us both. He would have waited for us to go to sleep and he would have shot us both. There is no doubt in my mind that he would have done that. I guess he had promised himself that he would not kill any of his kids after striking Randy in the head with a hammer. Even still, the next morning dad reminded us, when he asked me at least, how did I sleep? I knew it was a message.

However, him being in his sixties, wisdom prevailed and he allowed us to live. Over dad's assurances that he was cool, I packed my shit and went back to Texas. I had been home less than twenty four hours. However, I was young, so the eighteen hour drive back to Houston was doable. I was homeless for eleven days before Al, a college friend allowed me to move in.

My father died in the late 1980's and one of my brothers took my father's gun as a keepsake. While involved in a domestic dispute, my brother used my father's gun. The police eventually confiscated the gun and ran ballistics test on it. Police learned that there were three unsolved homicides attached to the gun. Dad had this gun for most of my life. But, I didn't need the California police to tell me about my dad.

I told the prosecutor about how Henry would beat the shit out of Susan and how she would call Wendell for protection. The prosecutor had some empathy for Wendell. When the prosecutor's dad died, I was one of the first people that called him with my condolences sharing with him that I too had lost my father. Of course, I didn't tell him that I thought that my dad was a sociopath. However, it was apparent to me that the prosecutor was very close to his dad, when his eyes welled up with tears.

Nonetheless, the prosecutor appreciated my condolences. Afterwards, he offered Wendell a plea bargain to Voluntary Manslaughter, a reduced count of Murder. To me, in my mind, this was better than the death penalty, life without parole or just life in prison with parole. Sadly, Wendell's uncle started talking shit to me because he didn't want Wendell to spend a day in prison for this murder. He wanted Wendell to walk away Scot –free claiming that the shooting was in self-defense.

I shared with him how Wendell traveled at least three miles through twenty-five traffic lights. How Wendell in that ten to fifteen minutes ride had time to calm down before he reached Susan's house. Now mind you, Wendell did tell Henry, I'm going to deal with you if he had to come over there again. And you know what, Wendell did. I told Wendell's uncle how a jury could see Wendell's action as premeditated murder.

But, you know how people are when they are not sitting at the table. They have the heart of a fucking lion. But if they are in fact sitting at the table, when it's their life hanging in the balance, they turn into pure pussy. You can see it in their eyes and that's what Wendell's uncle was to me, a pussy with Cognac on his breath. Eventually, Wendell took his medicine and went to prison. When Wendell got out of prison, he never called me, but that's cool. I knew that when Wendell was doing his time, he met a lifer or two that was his age or younger and in his heart Wendell thanked me. Wendell thanked me because he knew he was coming home.

I hope that in his soul Wendell and particularly Susan beg God for forgiveness. I hope Susan never involves her youngest son in her affairs. I hope that somebody tells Susan that her sons are not her men existing to fight her marital battles. Next time, bring home some decent dick. Better yet, go buy some toys. Batteries are sold separately.

Sentence: *Voluntary manslaughter five years to serve.*

OLD SPICE

"A man that finds a wife finds a good thing."
Proverbs 18:22

B obby had no business being here in the first place until he had finished his penal obligation with the state of Texas. He had at least three years left when he decided to jump parole, come to Atlanta and start his life all over again. Bobby had heard the stories like most African Americans about the opportunities in Atlanta and how progressive the black folks were. Bobby soon learned that it didn't matter that he had decided to straighten up and fly right or otherwise turn his life around. He failed to factor in the fact that people you invite into your life can keep up mess and otherwise fucked up, particularly women and their grown ass sons.

Bobby got here and was able to get two jobs when most people couldn't even get one. He had met Debra when she would come to the cleaners where he worked his nine to five. They began to flirt back and forth which lead to a date and within a year, Bobby and Debra was married. Bobby moved in to Debra's modest home and quickly asserted himself as the man of the house by paying all the bills and keeping change in Debra's pocket. Bobby knew that Debra had a son but it was almost like out of sight out mind, he was in prison.

They didn't discuss how life would be after Debra's son Fred Lee was released from prison. Bobby had a soft spot for Fred Lee since he had done some time too. Bobby and Debra made it through the honeymoon period of their relationship. They even settled in and sincerely enjoyed each other company. However, it didn't take long for things to change after Fred Lee was released from prison and came home to live with them.

Bobby, like most men became angry that Fred Lee, unlike him was content to party all night, sleep all day and eat up all the food in the house. Seemingly, Fred Lee didn't learn anything from jail other than to improve on how to be a better criminal. Bobby couldn't tell Debra shit about her no good son. Debra told Bobby to give the boy some time to get adjusted. She would say, I'm just glad my man is home.

We all know of examples where women have crossed the line in rearing their sons. They put added pressure on the child constantly reminding him at 5 years old that he is the man of the house. Sometimes, he's her only man. I shake when I think about the women that would willingly take me to their bedrooms in front of their teenaged or adolescent sons. At some point, the boy knows that I'm not really his uncle. Thus, I'm glad those incestuous comments have stopped. It only compounded the confusion for the kid of why some uncles slept with mom and others didn't.

Personally, I stop allowing myself to walk into bedrooms when the kids were up. If they weren't in bed when I got there, I wanted them to see me leave. Of course, I would double back. But still, why are some women so willing to allow their sons to see this? When I found myself in this predicament, I knew that I wasn't the only uncle she took to the bedroom. As I know, we all get lonely sometimes, but we still must think about the effect this will have on our sons.

In her day-to-day, she continues to disrobe in front of her son blurring the lines between mom, his adolescence and natural curiosity. Even more, if he is stuck with older sisters, it's just a matter of time before his sisters will begin to imitate their mom. Before, anybody peeps it, after awhile, he will too.

Soon, thereafter, Bobby felt like he was the one being pimped since no one worked in the house but him. To the contrary, Bobby had no say so about how shit was done. I knew how he felt. My dad would come home from work and fly into a rage if my brother and I were lying around when he came home from work. It was even worse if we had friends over or if we had drank all the Kool Aid. Then, we would really become some lazy motherfuckers laying around on him all day. Unlike Debra, my mother knew not to mumble a word or she would have hell to pay.

Bobby would make it home just after 11pm. Like most nights, he would have a beer, shower and go to bed. However, on this night when he laid in his bed something smelled funny. At first, he thought his mind was playing tricks on him. As he laid there the smell got stronger and stronger. Bobby finally asked Debra if she could smell the Old Spice in the sheets. At first, Debra lied and told him no, she couldn't smell no Old Spice in the sheets or anywhere else.

Bobby pushed the issue. Debra then told him that it was her new perfume before she said that Fred Lee had been in their bed. Perhaps, it was something that Fred Lee had on. Bobby replied in an accusatory tone, "So you do smell something." Bobby now upset asked her whose damn Old Spice was it. Bobby swore that he wore only Brut and he'd never dip himself in Old Spice. Debra lied and retracted her statement again saying that there was no Old Spice at all. Bobby said I thought you said it was something that Fred Lee was wearing or your new perfume.

As Bobby reached for her, Debra jumped out of bed screaming to the top of her lungs for Fred Lee. Fred Lee entered their bedroom and without question began to beat Bobby about the head with his fist. Fred Lee uttered repeatedly, "I'll kill you Nigga in here fucking with my momma." Fred Lee beat Bobby as if he were a child. Thereafter, he told Bobby, "If I ever catch you talking crazy to my momma, I'll kill you." Debra looked at Bobby like he got what he deserved for yelling at her about some damn Old Spice. Afterwards, she gave Bobby an ice pack to put on his head. For the first time, she told Bobby that Fred Lee was in prison for beating a police officer to the ground. Now, Bobby was officially put on notice not to fuck with her.

Bobby told me he felt like a damn fool. He's living in a house where he's paying all the bills and Debra's no good son put his hands on him. As if I doubted his masculinity, Bobby told me that he was man. I asked Bobby why he didn't call the police? Bobby said that he couldn't because he had skipped parole out of Texas and he would have been arrested. He claimed that Debra knew this and held it over his head. Feeling trapped, Bobby said that he wasn't going to run from the house where he pays all the bills and he wasn't going to take no more ass whippings from Fred Lee. So, Bobby started walking around the house with his .38 in his pocket.

For two days, Bobby walked around the house with his gun in his pocket and tried to reason with Debra. He told Debra that when they had problems she needed to keep Fred Lee out of it. He told her that the only thing that can happen is that Fred Lee would get hurt cause he wasn't taking no more ass whipping. Bobby wanted to know if Debra was having an affair. I guess from the look on my face, he said he knew that she was. He just couldn't believe that she would do it in his face. I asked him if she hadn't done in his face would it hurt any less. Bobby agreed with me.

Bobby's whole face and head were swollen. His eyes were filled with puss that crawled and matted itself in the corner of his eyes. The light blood that outlined the open wounds from Fred Lee punches decorated Bobby's face. I mean, he had fucked Bobby up. Bobby said yeah he got me pretty good. Very few middle-aged men have the wind and stamina to go toe to toe with a twenty five year old. I told Bobby he did what he could and that was all right. I know Bobby thought about killing Fred Lee that night. Bobby just didn't want to, and that was to his credit. Bobby had attempted to appeal to reason.

On Sunday, Debra had returned from church and Bobby again attempted to counsel with her on how they should argue more constructively and how important it was for her not to involve Fred Lee in their problems. Bobby believed that they could resolve everything amongst themselves without anyone getting hurt. Debra again started talking shit to Bobby about how she wasn't going to let him beat up on her over some bullshit. Bobby replied how he had never laid a hand her and that he wouldn't. Debra expressed how her son loved her and he would do anything to protect his momma. Bobby told her that was the point that they would only hurt each other when she involved Fred Lee.

As Debra danced about the kitchen cooking Sunday dinner, Bobby had purchased a six-pack of beer from the bootleg house and was sipping on his first one. Bobby told me that Debra seemed proud of the fact that Fred Lee whipped him. He told me how strange it was like Fred Lee was some knight in shinning armor. While conversing, Debra casually walked around the kitchen until she saw the gun print in Bobby's pocket.

What is that in your pocket? Bobby told her it was nothing. An anxious Debra began a rapid sequence of questions, "what you got that for?" "Who you gon shoot?" Bobby told Debra "I'm not gon shoot nobody, but I ain't taking no more ass whippings either." Before Bobby could explain himself, Debra screamed out for Fred Lee. "Fred Lee, Fred Lee! Bobby has a gun!" Fred Lee then ran in to the kitchen. He looked around to see where Bobby was standing and took a step back as if he was going to get his own gun. Bobby had his gun in his hand. Bobby told Fred Lee "I'm not going to shoot you but I ain't taking no more ass whippings." Fred Lee told Bobby "I told you what I was going to do if my momma called me again." Fred Lee lunged at Bobby. Bobby put him down with a shot to the chest. Fred Lee was dead.

Debra screamed and ran for Fred Lee as Bobby picked up his beer and what was left from the six-pack. He told Debra it was her fault. He had told her this would happen, as he left the house with his beer in his arms. Bobby had made it to the Texas state line before his car gave out. The Texas State Patrol found Bobby sitting on a picnic table at a rest stop. After they ran his identifiers, they arrested Bobby for the parole warrant out of Texas and the murder warrant out of Georgia.

The State Patrol Officer was so alarmed at the size of Bobby's head, he insisted on videotaping Bobby's face before placing Bobby in his patrol car. He said he didn't want anybody accusing him of beating Bobby during the arrest. I remember from the tape when he asked Bobby, "now you got this beating two days ago and your head is still swollen like this?" When Bobby replied, "Yeah, he got me pretty good."

At trial, I tried to get Bobby's case dismissed on a technicality. The state of Texas had so many days to return him to Georgia and Georgia had so many days of which to try Bobby for murder and they fucked up. I saw the evidence of the fuck up when they District Attorney showed me her file. By the time we went before the judge, the District Attorney had destroyed the evidence and the judge made me try Bobby's case before a jury. You should have seen Debra as she cried throughout her testimony upon every question asked of her by the crooked District Attorney. In between each answer, Debra just cried and blew the snot out of her nose. However, when it was time for me to ask questions, if Fred Lee were alive, she'd had Fred Lee beat my ass too.

I asked her if Bobby had told her about not involving Fred Lee in their disputes and she confirmed that he had. I asked her if she was as responsible as Bobby was for Fred Lee's death. Debra called me all kinds of motherfuckers with her eyes. She replied, no that she was not responsible and that the only person with a gun was Bobby. I asked her from the looks of how Fred Lee essentially beat Bobby's ass the first time it ain't like he needed a gun to do the job. Debra rolled her eyes away from me. I asked Debra why she would bring another man to her husband's bed. Debra told me she didn't. I asked how the Old Spice got there. The jury believed Bobby as he explained how this went down and they believed that Debra fucked around on him in their home. This was so, even after Debra got possessive and said she already had the home before she had married Bobby.

The Texas Police Officers testified how fucked up Bobby's head was when they found him on that picnic table several days after he fled Georgia. The cops Fred Lee had assaulted testified how violent Fred Lee was to them that eventually landed him in prison. After all of this, the jury found Bobby guilty of voluntary manslaughter. He was sentenced to twelve years in prison. I was happy with the outcome. Not only did we beat the life sentence without parole, we beat the life sentence that comes with the conviction for murder.

As time passed, I was able to get a friend, attorney Lucy Label to handle Bobby's appeal. Lacy was able to get the state of Texas to send her the documents that they had sent to the crooked District Attorney. The documents spoke for themselves. Georgia had failed to try Bobby's case in time. Afterwards, Lacy and the crooked District Attorney made a deal, Bobby was released from prison.

I bumped into Bobby on the street a few years back and he was still salty with me. He felt that I could have just as easily gotten those documents from Texas myself. Thus, I cost him two years in prison. Bobby was there when the judge denied my request for continuance regarding the Texas stuff. I guess I get no consideration from Bobby for finding him a new lawyer that knew how to obtain the stuff from Texas; the stuff that got him his life back. Let Bobby tell it, he should not have been punished at all and the fact that he was is my fault. Even though, I had not killed Fred Lee, he did.

PARENTAL SUPERVISION REQUIRED

Children

"You may give them your love but not your thoughts
for they have their own thoughts. You may house their
bodies but not their souls, for their souls dwell in the
house of tomorrow, which you cannot visit, not even
in your dreams."

Kahlil Gibran 1923

O n the news, you could tell his mother was attractive even as she mourned in a way that only a mother could. Police told her that it was her son David. He was dead. Police told her that David didn't do anything to provoke anybody. David wasn't doing anything wrong or stupid that drew attention to himself. Moreover, his death wasn't over money or drugs or a girl. David was killed because he was the next person to walk down the street to go to the party. Several bored teenagers agreed with an adult that they would attack the next person to walk down the street and it was David. Collectively, they beat and stomped him to death.

Atlanta stomped her feet to the ground in nothing short of outrage. At first, the misguided activists that make a living standing up for black folks assembled and complained. The activist complained because police put every kid from the party they could find on school buses. Police, in spite of parental outcry, would not allow the teens to leave until they got the information they needed regarding whom was responsible for David's death.

It was shameful how some parents reacted as to how the police did their jobs. The attitude was that it wasn't my child that died. For some, my child had nothing to do with it, so let them off the bus. Seemingly, the grief of David's mother was not enough to give other parents' cause or empathy for the temporary inconvenience of their own kids. Not, even, if it meant finding David's killers.

Atlanta was angry and confused at whom shall she be upset with. Where should she direct her anger? Should Atlanta be upset with David's mother for allowing him to go to the teen party? It seemed like every month a teen is killed at a teen party. Thus, it's always a risk to let your teen go and do what kids do. But, on the other hand, we can't keep our kids under house arrest forever. There comes a time when we have to and we must let them go and allow them to fly. It's nature.

Atlanta then began to ask about the parents of the teen killers. Where were they? What kind of people are they to rear a teen murderer; could they have done something to save their child before they killed someone else child? Should the parents be arrested and placed under a microscope to see where they fucked up in rearing their misguided children.

In the end, Atlanta decided to be upset with the teen murderers. She was shitty because of the ease and stupidity in their decision to kill another teen for kicks. As Atlanta stared at David's picture as it flashed across the television screen. Atlanta wondered had David not looked so feminine with his petite frame, light complexion and green eyes, if the murderers would not have been so quick to attack him. David's appearance of middle class living made it easy for them to follow through with their plan to attack the next person that walked down the street.

I was so upset with the whole thing sharing my outrage and frustration with anyone that would listen. At the same time, I remembered Scotty, who I had represented for doing the same thing fifteen years ago. Scotty was the adult, the older guy that hung around teenagers.

The teenagers looked up to Scotty, as most teenagers are quick to attach themselves to something or someone just to be seen. I looked at Scotty with the left eye of suspicion because he was every bit in his twenties hanging out with sixteen and seventeen years old kids.

I knew that Scotty was a dope boy that employed teens to sell his crack cocaine. He had purchased a nice home for himself in the prestigious Grant Park community in Southeast Atlanta, but he sold his junk over in the Bluff in Northwest Atlanta. Scotty at least had enough sense not to shit where he laid his head. I'm sure the good folks in Grant Park appreciated Scotty for that.

Scotty's crew had given some drugs to a forty year old man on consignment. When the man failed to pay on time, Scotty and a community of teenagers that worked for Scotty beat him with their hands and feet. The victim suffered severe blunt force head trauma which caused his death. One of the teens involved in the murder was Scotty's younger brother.

My wife had referred the case to me, when she introduced me to Scotty's mother. My wife being a criminal defense attorney as well was getting out of the game after many months of me begging her to do so. I saw Scotty's mom as a self-proclaimed church woman with hats that adorned her head as if she were the Queen of England or something. She was a big lady that wore glasses and dressed a lot older than what she was. Scotty's mom spoke of him as if he were her man.

I don't know how many times I asked my wife to do something else. I told her that she had nothing to prove to anyone and she didn't. Up until then, I was the only thing that had corrupted her life. I mean before we left Chicago, she worked as a lawyer for children. When one of her kids, Pookie was implicated in a murder of a white woman, the gangs killed him to assuage the pressure police put on the Chicago gangs for her murder. My wife mourned for that kid as if he was ours.

When we moved to Atlanta, it didn't take long for her to represent a Mr. Jones accused of robbing and raping a senior citizen. The state was seeking the death penalty. Mr. Jones left my wife a suicide note calling her an angel and telling her that she was better than this. Mr. Jones suggested that she do something else with her career before he hung himself with a sheet at the county jail. Not even his death was enough to get her to shift gears into another area of practice. Over my anger and sincere curiosity, she never allowed me to read the suicide note Mr. Jones had left her.

Finally, my wife came home one day. She didn't speak as she entered the house but simply disrobed and showered. I knew something was wrong. It wasn't uncommon for her not to speak to me because that's where we were in our marriage. But, this silence I had seen before. The silence you learn from someone you love. The silence that you can't explain but you know what it is when you see it, sort of silence.

So I asked my wife what was wrong. She hesitantly told me about her client she had visited at the county jail. She knew what it was, when she noticed that he was non-responsive to her questions and his hands remained in his lap underneath the table. Like in real time, it was too late for her to leave, when the convulsive expressions on his face triggered her recognition of his circumstances.

This all made her, the former Southern debutante feel dirty enough to come straight to the house and shower. Again, I became angry with her and almost jealous before I demanded that she find another practice area. Not one for embarrassment, I had even threatened to tell her parents of these events. At that point, she gave up criminal law and referred Scotty's momma to me.

Scotty's momma's, Ms. Melba was a card. As far as she was concerned, Scotty was innocent. Not that she was at the scene or a witness to anything, Scotty told her that he didn't do it and she believed him. Her kids wouldn't lie to her cause she raised them right. Ms. Melba acted shitty to me because I couldn't get Scotty out of jail on bond quick enough. Scotty being accused of murder was beside the point.

When I saw the news of David's death and how those parents reacted to their kids being placed on the school bus by police. I thought of Ms. Melba and her self-righteous indignation toward the dead forty year old crack head her boys along with others were accused of beating to death.

Ms. Melba would come by my office and scream at me before she would tell me what she was going to do. I frustrated her so much that she finally told me that I wasn't shit and I needed to be working at Sears. I would just look at her big-ass and imagine myself knocking that silly ass church hat off her head. She acted as if Scotty was her man.

Ms. Melba in her frustration with me called my wife and asked her to talk to me and she did. My wife essentially told me that I was making her look bad enough since she did marry me. At least, I could have gone to the crime scene by now. So, I did. Walter, an attorney friend of mine had grown up in the Bluff was to meet me there. The Bluff is to Atlanta as South Central is to Los Angeles; the Westside to Chicago; North Philadelphia; parts of Miami, 5th Ward in Houston or any other drug infested area in the United States.

Prescott and I had parked at the scene in his M3 BMW. Prescott and Walter each represented one of the teens. As Prescott and I walked around the scene oblivious to the indigenous folks that began to position themselves around us, Walter pulled up in his truck yelling just as loud as the preacher's kid he was greeting a cousin of his.

Walter got out of his truck and shook his cousin's hand. His cousin had relocated across the street from Prescott and I from the corner, where he was when we pulled up. Walter's cousin asked him if he knew us, and Walter replied that Prescott and I were his friends. Walter's cousin gave some sort of signal and the indigenous folks returned to the cracks and crevices they had emerged from.

Afterwards, Walter screamed at his cousin, "Wait a minute, ya'll were going to rob my boys?" Walter's cousin told him "Hell yeah." He told Walter that Prescott and I were slipping coming over to the Bluff acting all familiar. Walter's friendliness to his cousin turned to anger as he expressed the many ways he would kick his cousin's ass. As Walter inquired, "What the fuck you doing out here in the middle of the day anyway?" Walter then looked to me and asked, "Do you believe this shit?" Before he exclaimed, "I hate Niggas!" To Prescott and I, Walter snapped, "Ya'll get ya'll shit, let's go before I have to kill a motherfucker." Walter was known to carry a .forty and .9-millimeter caliber handguns.

It didn't take long for me to tell my wife and Ms. Melba that I put my life in danger for Scotty by going to the scene. In fact, we didn't find one witness that would talk to us. Ms. Melba simply said I didn't do anything I wasn't paid to do.

At trial, the state had the same issues with witnesses that Prescott and I had. No one from the neighborhood would come forward. In David's case police knew if they had let the teens go home, it was possible that no one would have come forward for David. However, teens from the bus identified the teens involved in David's murder. Consequently, three of the juveniles later confessed to their role in David's murder. The adult said he wanted a lawyer.

The District Attorney agreed with me that they had several problems proving who did what to the forty-year old crack-head victim. Thus, we struck a deal. Ms. Melba insisted that Scotty not do a day of time because he didn't do anything. Scotty thought differently. He was happy not to confront that life sentence staring him in the face for a murder conviction. Still, Ms. Melba told me I wasn't shit. To date, my ex-wife is an administrator at Spelman College. Walter disinvited his larcenous cousin from the annual family Christmas dinner.

Sentence: *Involuntary manslaughter 5 years to serve.*

CHAPTER THREE

EMASCULATION

I'M A MAN

Rome told them, "If I catch ya'll selling shit on my corners I'm going to deal with you." However, Rome never told them which corners were his. So, when Rome would find one of them working alone he would kidnap them at gunpoint, handcuff 'em and throw them in the trunk of his car. Rome would then drive to a not so remote location, open the trunk, remove them and cuff them around a tree. Rome would then beat them about the head with his gun until they were unconscious, pull their pants down and anally rape them. Rome got about three of them before they ambushed and killed him. After they killed him, they pissed and defecated on Rome's body. All of this shit occurred right down the street from my house. Thus, it was time to move.

The emasculation of a man can take on many forms or degrees. The most popular form of emasculation can be a psychological process, which usually involves a woman. Comparable to brainwashing, she convinces you that you have fallen short of her expectations. Cunningly, through her expert use of passive aggression over a period of time, she has you doubting yourself, as she has begun to doubt you. In an attempt to bargain with her, you find yourself compromising on shit that didn't matter in the first place. But, now has become a point of contention, when you're simply trying to get your dick sucked. In her deception, she refuses to tell you that she started fucking around on you long before she started complaining.

The worst form of emasculation is when a man rapes another man. The intent of the rape is to fuck you up psychologically. To put into question everything you were taught to be by your dad, institutions and society. To let you know, that you were fucked and can be fucked again because they see a weakness in you. Most men, don't have a fear of prison, they have a fear of being raped while in prison.

I believe that Rome got his motive and method from Cocoa, an ex-con that lived in a neighboring community of mine. Cocoa stood about 6'5", 255 lbs and carried it like a middle linebacker. His thing was to sell you hits of crack and then beat your ass and take it back before he'd rape you. My friend Walter Robinson's client finally killed Cocoa after such an attack. The good news was that Walter also represented one of the young men that killed Rome. Thus, Walter had experience with this sort of thing.

Walter said that Cocoa had at least 7 male rapes to his credit, but the only person that reported Cocoa to police was a middle class white guy. The white guy had gone over to the ghetto to buy some crack. Cocoa sold him the crack and then raped him. When he reported the rape to police, they laughed and told him that's what you get. So, in his embarrassment, he no longer pursued the charges.

Sadly, word had it that Cocoa had AIDS. Walter client's was found not guilty after a bench trial by a judge. The judge reprimanded the District Attorney for bringing Cocoa's murder case to court as if society owed Cocoa some justice. Thus, Cocoa was a motherfucker that deserved killing. Certainly, he was not a victim that had clean hands.

In our case, Walter's client, Chuck had been maimed in an unrelated shooting that all but destroyed his right arm, which made it virtually impossible for him to fire a gun. He and my client, Hooker Jenkins along with three others were charged with shooting Rome to death. Chuck was one of the guys that Rome had kidnapped and thrown in the trunk of his car, but Chuck was able to escape. With his fucked up arm, Rome was unable to handcuff Chuck. At least, that what he told Walter.

When I first met Hooker, he simply told me that he didn't shoot anybody, but he wasn't sad the Nigga was dead. I asked, "Were the police reports accurate?" He said "there was a lot of stuff left out." As we continued to talk, Hooker never told me that Rome had raped his friends. Even, more, the rape information was not contained in the police reports. Hooker at least for now was prepared to keep his friends secrets from me. Moreover, if it came out that Rome had fucked his boys, it wasn't coming from him.

On one hand, I admired his loyalty to his friends. On the other hand, I'm reminded of how a false sense of obligatory friendship can set in motion one irreversible bad decision after another. So, I asked Hooker, if it was okay for me to speak with his mother. Hooker was only nineteen years old no more than twenty. Hooker said it was cool. I don't recall ever speaking with his mother nor do I recall a phone call from her.

The police reports mentioned that five male blacks ambushed the victim under a pretext of a drug deal, which was essentially true. What the police reports failed to say was that five male blacks angry over the serial rapes of their friends got together and hatched a plan of revenge, which included murder. Miles Jefferson's client called Rome and asked him to meet him up at the KFC parking lot for a drug deal near Turner Field. The KFC was literally a block away from Rome's house. In fact, Rome could see the KFC sign from his back porch.

When Rome walked out of his front door presumably on his way to make the deal, he was shot down in front of his house. Allegedly, Walter's client then shitted on Rome and Bousuant Prioleau's client pissed on him. I imagined that Walter's client failed to think ahead and bring some wet wipes for the occasion. I guess he felt the overwhelming need to emasculate Rome by shitting on his dead body as Rome might have emasculated him in life.

Police rounded up the five men based on talk in the neighborhood of who may have had a problem with Rome. The five men charged with Rome's murder ranged in age from 18 to 23 years old. Even, more, none of the five would identify the shooter. When I confronted Hooker about the anal sex, he denied that he was a victim. Hooker said, "I'm a man," in a way like he was more of a man than his friends that had been raped at gunpoint by Rome.

Besides Walter, Miles, Prioleau and I, there was Norwood Brooks a former District Attorney. Brooks was a man conflicted by his work and life. He grew up in Michigan but gave you the impression that he had never been around educated black folks. When Brooks actually met an African American that was as intelligent or smarter, he was already an adult male. Brooks did not know how to process this life fact of "intelligent black folks" since he was always taught that he was somehow better than most. Thus, his delusional confusion of the supposed order of things pored over into his personal life. Brooks was a suicide survivor or one that just threatened suicide for attention. However, you cut it, Brooks had some serious problems.

When Atlanta elected its first African American District Attorney there was white flight from the District Attorney's Office. Nancy Grace had decided to move on before she was picked up by CNN. Some say she benefited from the O.J. Simpson trial more than anybody. For me, she served as a barometer of how much hatred still stewed in the hearts of America. America acted as if all black people were pulling for O.J. Simpson. The African American community acted as if O.J. being acquitted served as poetic justice for every black man that was wrongfully convicted. To me, it was the silliest time in American Jurisprudence. I said all of this to say, Brooks should have left the District Attorney's Office when the others fled. However, to another District Attorney Circuit because defending the rights of others was not in his blood.

I can recall how Brooks disliked me so much, that when he was a prosecutor he made a deal with the actual murderer to testify against my client. Attorneys Prescott Williams, Walter Robinson and I represent three brothers and their friend charged with murder.

Brooks gave the friend, the actual shooter, a deal to testify against the brothers. When Brooks discovered that he had fucked up, it was too late and the brothers walked a few years through the prison doors and were released. On the defense side, Brooks and I represented co-defendants. Again, the shooter confessed and accepted all responsibility for the murder. Brooks convinced his client to take the witness stand and implicate himself after it was clear he would walk on murder charges. In my opinion, Brooks was responsible for his client's conviction.

Like I said, Brooks was a confused man and was a defense attorney out of necessity rather than passion. Bousuant was from Chicago and was the typical proto-type public defender. Easily intimidated, Bousuant was never really prepared for trial. He was so busy with so many cases, he would perform to the level of minimum competence just to ensure a client of a fair trial, but he added no mustard. Trial attorneys are just like any other profession, there's the average, good, better and best. In Texas we'd say you get what you paid for just like anything else. It didn't help that Bousuant's approach to trial was just as plain and monotonous as a Catholic nun at a convent during quiet time.

See, as a public defender, Bousuant didn't have time to go the extra mile. He had other clients waiting on their day in court. Personally, I liked Bousuant but was disappointed that he compromised what I thought he could do for so many, because he never stood up and said enough, "I can only do so much at a time." To the contrary, I'm sure he cared about his client as evidenced, when he took yeast to a client at the County Jail. When the client was busted for making toilet beer, he told on Bousuant and he was nearly disbarred. I, on the other hand won't give a client a cigarette for a quarter. The only yeast I've ever paid for was a honey bun if a client purchased one from the money I left on his books from commissary.

At trial, we were before the elegant Judge Deneaux. She was smart, attractive and dare I say sexy. I don't think that I was her type, but I could have been. Judge Deneaux had a medium brown complexion with LPH (long pretty hair) to her shoulders. Her teeth were perfect.

One could assume that she didn't drink coffee because her teeth were so white. She stood about 5'6" with heels and she knew she was fine. To the contrary, I could never make her laugh. I know my gallows humor borders on appropriate, but if we can't laugh about this shit who can.

Walter told Judge Deneaux about the facts of the case. Walter, the preacher's kid seemed to preach and cite scripture whenever he recited facts for judge or jury. When he finishes, you have to check yourself because you'd say Amen. Then, he'd explain the meaning of Amen as a Hebrew word meaning, etcetera. As he explained the facts to Deneaux, I think Walter was trying to be nastier than what was necessary; but how can you clean up being handcuffed to a tree, pistol whipped and anally raped by a man.

To say that she was outraged is an understatement. My long time friend was the prosecutor. It was just a matter of sport for him to see if he could convict everybody until Judge Deneaux intervened. Rhetorically, speaking, she said, in a black woman's voice, "I know you're not going to prosecute them boys after what he did to them?" The scowl on her face as she addressed the prosecutor was clear. If he had said yes, Deneaux was going to give us as much latitude in discussing those sex acts committed by Rome as she could.

The prosecutor finally relented and cut, Miles, Walter and I out of the trial. Hooker's County Jail time was commuted to time served and he was released. Walter and Miles' clients received walk away sentences as well. However, I don't know why Bousuant and Brooks clients went to trial. Within the week, they both were convicted of murder. I didn't go to the trial but Walter did. Walter called both Brooks and Bousuant some sorry excuses for lawyers and they needed to go back to where they came from. I told Walter that I was trained in Chicago. He said I could stay, as if I needed his permission.

Sentence: *Life in prison.*

NEW SHOES

I laughed until I cried. I just couldn't control myself after what I had just heard. Police found Clifton hiding underneath a bridge and arrested him for the murder of his sister in law and the attempted murder of his estranged wife. I had managed to make it to the jail before police had bathed and jump-suited Clifton. When they brought him out, I saw the dust, dirt, leaves and shit still in his hair. His elbows were as white as rust and stood out as indication of the dry night air he had slept in. After they sat Clifton in the booth, I just looked at him in silence and didn't say a word. Uncomfortable with the silence, Clifton said that he didn't know why he was locked up and the police was treating him so aggressively. I began to laugh out loud and after a minute or two, so did Clifton.

Clifton tried to play crazy with me. How ironic, me, the guy that has tried to get people to act crazy for a living. We laughed for several minutes first at the dirt and dust in his hair and then we laughed at the leaves that littered Clifton's body. Just when we thought we were done, we'd start laughing again. Clifton laughed so hard he farted in my presence before we laughed again. Thereafter, I looked at Clifton like he was the guy that paid too much for what he got and now he could pay the cost of his decisions with his life.

A few days ago, I had told Clifton that if I got him out of jail, don't go do some O. J. shit. He promised that he wouldn't. He told me that he was through with his wife and it was over. Clifton had moved here from South Florida. He was a childhood friend of my college roommate, Casper King, who was an attorney in Houston, Texas. Clifton's mom was in need of my services because Clifton had been accused of beating and stalking his wife, Rene.

Clifton's sister, Katy had gotten him a job at a food distribution center, where she had worked over ten years. He worked a few months before he sent for Rene and their four kids. Clinton had a pair of fourteen year old twin boys. It didn't take long before Clifton and Katy got Rene a job at the center. Rene from the looks of it had never traveled much and loved Atlanta on the few occasions she had visited. For Rene, Atlanta soon became her new shoe store. Atlanta has longed had the reputation of a home wrecker and it wasn't long before Rene tried on some new shoes.

A number of married couples that have come to Atlanta ended up divorce. I fell victim to Atlanta as well. I remember a fellow attorney of senior years asked me how long had I been here. At the time, I had only been here three months. The attorney told me that he would give me a year with my wife. I was offended as I should have been at his prediction. I thought that this motherfucker doesn't know me. A few months later, I saw the veteran attorney at a restaurant where I was having breakfast with a friend. He looked at me and smiled before he lowered his head into his coffee. If I wasn't guilty, I certainly acted as if I was.

For the first time in her life, Rene was making over thirty thousand dollars a year. While in Florida, she was stuck being a single mom working bull shit jobs to keep the lights on and kids fed. But now Rene was soon to be a victim of Atlanta in more ways than one. Thus, Rene was in a new city with a new job, a new life and she was about to find some new shoes.

I don't know if Rene looked for the new shoes on the job or if the shoes just snuck up on her. Sometimes, when you're in the same environment everyday with someone that's attempting to be and look their best, it's hard not to notice and on occasion find them attractive. Whenever it happened, Rene had found some shoes that she liked. Rene had found romance right there on the job. At first, it started out as a casual wear thing because of her circumstances before it progressed to a regular one. Other than the fact that Rene was married, the only other problem was that she, Clifton, Katy and the new shoes all worked at the same place.

Katy tried to figure out how to handle Rene's infidelity as gently as she could. On the other hand, she knew Clifton and how violent he can be. Katy figured that this was her backyard. Moreover, that both Rene and Clifton got hired on the strength of her word. Likewise, Katy soon came to regret getting her folks hired. Even more, would it be better for her to tell Clifton what everybody is talking about at the water cooler or let him find out on his own. Eventually, Katy got tired of people laughing behind Clifton's back, so she told him.

After Katy told Clifton, he reacted just like she thought he would. Clifton came home from work and whipped Rene's ass. By 11p.m., he was in jail. By 11 a.m., the next morning, I was having the macho man talk with Clifton. I told Clifton to let Rene go and that he could do better. I told him that she had moved on and so must he. I personally wouldn't want her ass after she'd fucked around in my face on the job. Even though I had never seen her, I started to tell him how ugly Rene was before I caught myself. Casper had told me that Rene was unattractive before I got Clifton out of jail the first time.

In the past, I have given the macho man talk to friends and they ended back up with their girlfriends. On one occasion, I was demoted from the wedding party. On another occasion, I was shamed because the girl thought I was a mutual friend. She had asked me how I could talk about her stuff like that having never had the privileged of trying it for myself. My high school buddy told me to mind my own damn business before our relationship was strained for several years. In spite of these not so well experiences, I thought Clifton needed someone to signify and understand his pain. But, at the same time, give him strength and a different point of view.

I told Clifton that he may have to wait ten days before he is released from jail. O.J.'s verdict had a ripple effect here in Georgia, where people accused of domestic violence were required to stay in jail at least ten days before they were released. They called it a cooling down period, I called it District Attorney Time. However, no one wants to release a person on a domestic charge and later learn that they in fact killed the object of their affection.

Clifton promised me that he was over, through, and otherwise done with his wife. Clifton seemed so calm and reflective as we bonded. We began to talk about our mutual friend Casper King and basketball. Clifton seemed cool to me. He appeared to be okay. So, I approached the prosecutor and told her my version of the facts and for the most part I told the truth. I may have told her that Rene fucked two guys on the job when in fact, it was only the one. But, hell, one was enough. The prosecutor asked me if Clifton was cool and I told her he was. I told her that Clifton was friends with a mutual friend of mine. The prosecutor gave Clifton the credit that I had with her and let him out of jail. Clifton's only restriction was to have no contact with his trifling ass wife.

Within a day or two, Rene had given Clifton some sympathy pussy. Within the same week, she put Clifton back on pussy rations and threatened to have him arrested for violating the protective order. For Rene, things were great. She could continue to wear her new shoes and when she was running low, she could call on Clifton. It didn't take long after Clifton returned to work, that the conversations behind his back got louder and louder.

One day Clifton asked Rene if he could come over and she told him yes but later changed her mind. Like most men, Clifton's mind began to race and he thought he had been bumped by the guy on the job. Rene sensing Clifton was pissed off became concerned and asked her sister Melody to spend the night. Melody was only a few years older than Rene. I had met Melody years ago because she worked as the concierge in a Buckhead high rise where a friend of mine lived. I found Melody to be a pleasant and nice enough person. But, I didn't know Melody and Rene were sisters until after she was dead.

On the night in question, Melody agreed to sleep on Rene's sofa and Rene's 14 year old twins went to their room, and the younger kids went to their rooms. Rene had gotten ready for bed and the house was quiet before Melody heard someone playing with the locks at the front door. Clifton had never surrendered his keys to the house and I guess he decided to come see for himself. I guess he wanted to catch Rene in the act. Which, I thought was rather sadistic if not freaky. I wouldn't want to see the object of my affection bent over or sideways by another man. Call me immature, I never asked a lover how she likes it. Such questions provide me with disturbing images and too much insight into her pussy resume. To the contrary, I've never had one that didn't eventually tell me anyway.

As Clifton entered into the house, a waiting Melody whacked his ass with a metal baseball bat. She didn't say anything that would ward off an intruder, Melody just waited with that bat she had placed next to the sofa just in case Clifton showed up. When Clifton was struck with the bat, he screamed, dropped his gun and grabbed his arm. Before, Melody could strike him again, Clifton fatally shot her in the chest with his other gun. Clifton then walked upstairs to a hysterical Rene. As she began to beg and plead with Clifton to spare her for the sake of the kids, he placed a pillow over her stomach, two shots to the abdomen. After he noticed Rene was still alive, he placed the pillow over her chest before he heard the screams of his kids "Daddy don't kill our Momma." Clifton caught himself and fled. For two days, Clifton hid underneath a highway bridge and that's where police found him.

A few days later, I found myself at the hospital. I knew that Rene was to be released that day so I decided to go visit Rene and offer her a ride home if she needed one. I mean if new shoes was going to pick her up that was fine with me. But, something told me that she was on her own because I knew if she wasn't just a piece of pussy for new shoes before, she certainly was now.

Professionally speaking, I've never felt so low in my career, if not my life. I mean I knew that Rene needed a ride home and I could have provided just that but I didn't. I went further, I tried to convince her that some how things were not as bad as they seemed. The hypocrisy of it all is that I quietly blamed Rene just as much as I blamed Clifton. It was Rene that brought her sister into her mess that caused Melody her life. To me, it was as if Rene pulled the trigger herself.

Rene knew that Clifton wouldn't be able to handle the rations with knowledge that someone else on the job was now tasting the shaky pudding he taken for granted for so long. I convinced myself, that it was Rene's greed and lust that set this murderous rampage in motion. It was Rene that tried to juggle the old with the new and everybody knows that all shoes don't fit the same.

In my representation of Clifton, I was made aware that he coached his one son's baseball team. One twin was gay, and Clifton was not too keen on that but no one told me of any bashing. Clifton was a hard worker that liked a beer after work and thought he still had what he had in South Florida with Rene. Perhaps, it would have been, until he learned the hard way as so many others have; that most young couples cannot move to Atlanta and remain married. The secret is that you have to wait until you get here for matrimony.

As I pushed Rene down the hospital corridor, I felt ashamed of myself. I even felt dirty. In my self-centeredness, I learned how much of an insincere bastard I can be. I saw how low I could crawl. Clifton didn't deserve this from me. Clifton had entered Rene's house with two guns. He was there to kill everybody including himself, but he couldn't kill his kids as they stared him in the face. He just couldn't do it. I mean who takes two guns to a crime scene when one is more than enough for the job. Clifton had snapped into a jealous homicidal rage, but that nigga wasn't crazy. He was just mad. So he went to Rene's prepared to kill her because he figured that he had given her too much for her to share with others. He went to kill her because she made him feel like a fool over some new shoes.

Hence, here I am pushing Rene down the hospital corridor going the extra mile for a jealous fool. I'm going the extra mile after someone was senselessly killed. I know I will have to pay for this walk with a stain on my soul. Lord please forgive me for I have sinned the sin of egotism and arrogance. For my egotism, why would I engage in this manipulative behavior for a homicidal stranger? Certainly, I didn't do it for the money or out of genuine concern or sympathy for Rene. I admit that I did it to plant the seed of forgiveness for an unforgettable act. In my arrogance, this went beyond doing my job, I made it personal.

This inner need to win, to set the stage for success is what's expected of me and what I was paid to do. I mean I would want someone to do the same for me. Deep down inside the feeling of taking a fucked up situation and making it better is a motivation I can't explain. Seemingly, I'll almost do anything to achieve what I want. Interestingly, enough, this attitude of achievement applies in my personal life as well. The emotional struggle for me is that no matter how bad the circumstances or what's at stake, how low I would go to come up. I know this need to win makes me emotionally dangerous, if not reckless.

By the time we made it to our first court appearance, Rene was called to the stand for the purpose of bond. She told the court why she didn't want Clifton released from jail. Rene said she feared for her life. I essentially told the court that she had found some new shoes and she didn't want Clifton around anymore. I confronted her with how she'd call him up and give him a taste when she was running low, but would threaten him with jail whenever new shoes came around. Clifton's mother and Katy were so impressed with me. They didn't know I had enough "shit" in me to deal with an angry Rene. Besides, I wasn't the only one that accused her of killing Melody. I heard Rene's own mother took the same position. In south Florida, everyone knew that Clifton had homicidal tendencies, so Rene should have played the situation better.

The judge denied Clifton a bond and the veteran prosecutor put me on notice that he had a cocktail ready for Clifton. He told me that he would have Clifton's file ready to certify as a death penalty case in a few weeks. The state was planning on juicing Clifton for his murderous rampage. I mean I couldn't even argue that Clifton didn't try to kill Rene, shit he shot her twice.

The prosecutor had been around for over thirty years. He was a distinguished, handsome, middle-aged man rather professorial in his approach, but mean as hell. One could get the impression that he had tried to fit in with the black middle class and the white boys that run Atlanta. At one time, he had run for District Attorney of Atlanta, but had lost. The word was that he had offended too many of the right people to have such a position. In spite of all the chivalry, tradition and progress, Atlanta is still fighting the civil war. It seemed the prosecutor didn't know whose team he was on, so both sides kept the door closed on him, which made him bitter and loyal to no one.

The prosecutor and I had tried a few murder cases before in Atlanta, where he was prominent before he lost the election. During one of those trials, it was around Thanksgiving, he had mentioned to me that he wanted some chittlins, but did not want to risk being seen purchasing them in his bourgeois black neighborhood. He told me how he drove over twenty miles one way to the ghetto to buy a ten pound bucket and avoid detection. He shared with me how ashamed he was of himself. I sat there and listened, as I tried to figure out why he was sharing such a story with me. Did he assume correctly, that I would go to the heart of the high rent district to buy my hog guts and he admired my gumption? For some reason, I felt badly for him or any man that's conflicted within himself.

I called Casper King my former college roommate and friend that referred Clifton's case to me. I told him that the state had certified Clifton's case as a death penalty. Casper began to tell me that as kids how Clifton enjoyed killing stray cats and dogs for fun. Alarmed at this information, I knew that Clifton was a killer based on FBI studies that found a pattern of homicide begins with the killing of small animals in childhood.

A few months later, I told Clifton that I was having trouble finding folks in Atlanta to testify on his behalf. In all of our conversations, Clifton came off like he had a right to shoot Melody because she hit him with a bat. Moreover, he had a right to shoot Rene for sleeping with another man. I told him that since new shoes wasn't in the house when you shot Rene that argument wasn't going to work. Finally, I told him that if Melody had shot and killed your ass, she would not have spent one day in jail. Clifton you broke into the house. Based on these conversations, I knew Clifton was on some bullshit. I knew Clifton was an unrepented killer.

After I received the state's witness list, I saw that Clifton's fourteen years old twins were set to testify against him. I asked him if he wanted to take a deal as opposed to taking his kids through this shit. Clifton told me no and asked me whose team I was on. I asked him if I were on your kids' team would that make me a bad person or lawyer. Clifton sat quietly and thought about what I had said before he said no. Good, I told him I quit. Subsequently, I found Clifton another lawyer and gave him the attorney's fees. Thereafter, Clifton pled guilty to Melody's murder and to the attempted murder of Rene. Clifton was the first person that I represented and got out of jail for assaulting his lover only to return and attempt to kill her. Clifton tried to do some O.J. shit after he promised he wouldn't. In my naiveté, I thought the macho man speech worked. I know that I rationalized this shit away. I tell myself that this murder had nothing to do with me, but was between Clifton and God. The fact is, even if I'm right, it doesn't make me feel any better. All of this over some new shoes.

Sentence: *Life without the possibility of parole.*

I'M JUST SAYING

I don't know what I would do if I encountered someone that victimized me in such a horrible manner. I mean that is an age old question, what would you do if you encountered someone that raped your wife or killed a love one and they got away with it? The law or a jury of their peers found them not guilty of something they did to you or yours. I wouldn't be the first to say that revenge is like lust, we all have a little of each inside of us. Revenge and lust realized is nothing more than immediate pleasure that doesn't last long enough and gives us some sense of guilt after the act is done.

Jason had walked around for thirty-something years with revenge in his heart. Over the years it had been put to sleep deep inside of his heart. Perhaps, Jason on occasion had forgotten about his want of revenge in his search for normalcy, whatever that is. However, Jason's want of revenge was not a random thing. Seemingly, Jason was reminded that he had a score to settle, when Melvin his co-worker told Jason that he was going to fuck him. Moments later, Jason took a knife from the restaurant kitchen where both men worked and entered into the locker room. There waiting was a naked Melvin with his dick swinging in the wind talking about it was time. Jason stabbed Melvin thirty nine times.

The District Attorney called me out. He said that he was tired of people using the gay defense theory as an excuse to kill people. The District Attorney even called me a gay basher in the local newspaper.

I don't recall the newspaper calling me for a comment for my side of the story. So, there it was, I'm labeled a gay basher.

Had the newspaper asked me about Jason, I would have told them that he had been molested for as long as he could remember. I would have told them that Jason could not use the bathroom alone until he was 8 years old because he was so physically and emotionally fucked up. Jason had lived his ambiguous life confused as to who he was because he had been raped so much. My guess was that more than one person had abused Jason. He wouldn't tell me by whom.

Now, Jason was a man and the thought of someone fucking him again against his will was too much to bear. I can imagine that men go through the same process as women when they have been violated. They look at themselves to see if it was something about them that indicated "victim" on their foreheads. Was there a sign the attacker could sense in them, a sense of weakness or vulnerability that stood them out amongst the rest?

Victims I'm sure go through the process of trying to understand why someone, a living person did such a horrible thing to them. A refusal to believe that a loved one, an adult would victimize me and rob me of my innocence, in the name of perverted lust. Jason's denial soon turned to anger. His anger toward all those who should have looked out for him but didn't. Jason was angry with the many people that sexually abused him and angry with the unknown, because of his lack of coping skills to deal with his frustration.

Jason's depression went undetected and undiagnosed for years. As with most poor people, tragedy is just one more thing to deal with. Most black folks remember no matter what the ailment, gunshot wound or nail in your foot, your mother used the same medicine for both, rubbing alcohol. Hence, baby Jason just had to live with the fact that someone repeatedly fucked him as a child and got away with it. As a man, Jason would tell himself never again.

As Jason matured he eventually learned to put his molestation on a shelf somewhere. I don't think it's something that is ever placed behind you. Instead, you learn to live with it and assimilate with others as an adjusted person knowing full well that you're fucked up on so many different levels. But, you can't tell the world your secret. If you did, the world would victimize you again. She would perceive you as weak and less than what you are and what you would like to be. So you walk around with this nasty little secret that was conceived by another and has consumed your heart for so long. Secrets that you think about every living day when you simply encounter a woman you're smitten with.

The preoccupations of wondering if you're good enough or can she smell your abuser's dick on you. Thus, find you less than a man. I felt Jason's pain and frustration, as he told me his story. It was a relative of Jason's that first told me about Jason's abuse. Jason then confirmed as much and added some details of his childhood of abuse.

I'm not surprised that Jason opened up only after he was comfortable with me not judging him. I told Jason that it wasn't his fault. He was only a defenseless child, but it was like talking to a wall. To me, Jason had emotionally imprisoned himself a long time ago. For those that knew of his abuse and did nothing to protect him, Jason despised them. On the other hand, he loved them because they were the only family he had ever known.

On my many visits with Jason, I knew that Jason was trying to find peace and self-acceptance. On his off-day, Jason came to work to help out with a special party. He was to be married later on that evening and was expected to only work a few hours before he killed Melvin. Perhaps, being a husband was the validation of manhood Jason needed. He would not have been the first molested man that married and worked through his abusive past. I mean, the mind can carry around a violent imagination yet injure no one and live free of revenge. I do it all the time. To the contrary, one doesn't have to be sexually molested to have been abused. Revenge crosses over many genres of life and events that leads to wasted time. The time spent with the preoccupation of the death of others.

At trial, I don't know exactly what I said or how I came off. I do know that I didn't give a fuck about Melvin and that was clear. My disdain for Melvin was personal. I had pulled his criminal history and saw where he had been accused and convicted of raping a woman twenty years ago. Melvin had served some time in prison for that offense. Therefore, you rape a woman you'd rape a man. Particularly, if sex is just your thing and the power trip that attaches itself to rape is ambivalent to gender. Sadly, I couldn't find the woman Melvin had raped so the jury never got to hear that information.

The lead detective that testified at trial came off as if Jason was a sociopath and engaged in an unprovoked killing. He told the jury how Jason was attempting to mop up Melvin's blood as it spilled into the kitchen area from the locker room with his tee shirt. The jury looked around at each other as if Jason's behavior was bizarre if not irrational, and it was.

The medical examiner testified as to the stab wounds he counted being careful not to count the same wound twice. I asked him about rage killings. The prosecutor objected to his testimony as outside the scope of the medical examiner's area of expertise. The judge allowed the medical examiner to explain what a rage killing was. He essentially defined it in layman terms, "When a person repeats behavior that results in death even after death has occurred."

Jason attempted to explain to the jury why he did what he did. Not being very educated, it was difficult for him to explain himself. Jason didn't recall how many times he had stabbed Melvin. He claimed that he simply remembered the first and the last one. Moreover, Jason did not want to fully disclose his life of abuse and the effect it had on him. Sadly, Jason wanted a little or some pride at a time his humility was needed. I'm not saying that Jason would have rather gone to prison because of his pride. I'm just saying that he was not sophisticated enough to explain the emotional effect his repeated childhood rapes had on his adult life; a life that would have warranted empathy from a jury.

Essentially, the state accused me of gay bashing and argued that I was all for gay people going to hell anyway. The District Attorney didn't know me or the people that have influenced my life. There was no way for the District Attorney to have known that Bump, my neighborhood bully was suspected of being gay. Bump was like an older brother to me. A playground football and high school track star, Bump was my mentor. Even today, I love and look up to Bump as I did as a snotty nose kid. All of my life Bump was and remains fearless. Even in all of his perceived gayness, everybody knew not to fuck with Bump. I admired the respect that people gave him.

The District Attorney argued that he would rather Jason go free than to be found guilty of anything less than murder. When I attempted to tell the jury to put themselves in Jason's shoes, the District Attorney objected. The judge told them not to consider what I had just said. The judge even struck my comments from the record as they were illegal. I knew that my comments were illegal. I said them anyway. I was looking for any edge I could get for Jason. However, none proved helpful.

Sadly, no one from Jason's family came to court to testify for him not even his wife to be. Again, Jason was on his own and the people he loved the most fucked him again in their absence. At least this time, Jason spoke up for himself. I hope that he can accept whatever comes his way. I believe, at the end of the day, we all want to go out fighting for something, if not ourselves.

It didn't take long for the jury to convict Jason of murder. I would see the arrogant lead detective around the courthouse and he would gloat about his conviction as if it were his first one, virgin. I told him, had Jason stabbed Melvin only thirty eight times opposed to the thirty nine, we would have kicked his ass. We laughed before he told me to, "Get the fuck out of here." I told him to put yourself in Jason's shoes, what if that had happened to you. I'm just saying.

Sentence: *Life in prison.*

CHAPTER FOUR

IDENTITY

FORGIVENESS

I told her that I would get her out of jail. I told her that the money didn't matter. She deserved a second chance. I sincerely tried. I gave more than the college effort or more than most would have given the circumstances. Fortunately, I do not measure myself with someone else's yardstick. If I did overly concern myself with the opinions of others, I know that I would never be the best that I could be or obtain any level of emotional stability. My faith would be held in the hands of others, who may not have their shit together. So this thing, it was about me and what I said I was going to do and I failed. Every day, I think of her. I don't know how I became so emotionally involved with Misty but I did and in a way I began to feel sorry for her.

As an adult, like the next guy, I've had my share of life experiences where shit just didn't work out. The lies I was told as a child that if I worked real hard things would go my way. To the contrary, no one ever told me about the exceptions. The exceptions where things were different for those who had money, that things were different for those who knew the right people, the exception of race and gender. I know that I'm better off for not having being told of the exceptions. Perhaps, knowing of the exceptions would have stunted my growth because I would not have tried as hard to succeed. Thus, I just hope that my cynical attitude can be better explained by folks who attempt to describe me to others.

I don't know if anyone other than teachers, preachers, lawyers and medical doctors that are in the business of giving others hope every day. For me, it's a daunting task. I believe I'm of a dying breed. I still believe in second chances, the magic of rainbows and silver linings. To be able to give someone hope is a beautiful thing. Especially, if what was promised was realized. On the contrary, when the hope you've promised fails to manifest the reality can be harsh. My failure to deliver on my promise still has Misty serving a life sentence for murder. This is real hard for me. Even though I didn't put her there.

When I met Misty she had been convicted of murder and her appeal had been denied. The only legal remedy she had left was a writ of habeas corpus and her daddy hired me to file one. When she was about fifteen years old, Misty was dating a twenty-seven year old man named Blue. A chronic runaway, Misty stayed in the streets because she was tired of the beating inflicted on her by her self-proclaimed minister father. She also told me she was angry because her mother never intervened to save her.

I knew what Blue was just from reading the file. If I'm sure about anything, Blue was preparing Misty for a life on the street before she killed him. Misty shot Blue because he had given her a sexually transmitted disease and was arrogant about it. When she confronted Blue that her stuff was itchy, he punched her in the face. Later that week after Misty medically confirmed her condition at the clinic. She confronted Blue again and again he punched her in the face. Misty soon told her friend Tammy about her condition and how Blue would hit her as if she were a man.

Tammy arranged to get Misty a gun from the streets. Misty called Blue to come pick her and Tammy up to run an errand. As they got into Blue's car, Misty sat in the front seat and Tammy got in the backseat behind Misty. Misty brought up her condition to Blue, this time in front of Tammy. Blue slapped Misty in the face. In a cause and effect reaction, Misty shot Blue in the head in a moving car. The car ended up in an old man's yard. When police interviewed the man, he told them that he observed two teenage girls running from the car. It didn't take long before police arrested the fifteen years old Misty laughing hysterically from the back seat of the police car. Misty was charged as an adult for the murder of Blue. Tammy took a plea bargain and testified against Misty. Tammy gave the District Attorney all the evidence of premeditation he needed to secure a conviction of murder against Misty. Thus, it didn't take long for the jury to convict Misty and she was sentenced to life in prison. The jury heard little to no evidence that she was being molested by Blue or that he had given her a sexually transmitted disease. Personally, I felt it would have mitigated what she had done to his nasty ass.

I would drive at least one hundred miles one way to visit with Misty. On my first visit, I saw this beautiful caramel brown girl barely nineteen years old, with her hair in a bun. She had a wonderful smile and I remember her being polite to me. I gleaned that she appreciated my intelligence and my appearance because in future visits, she would tell me that I was getting fat and she liked the slimmer me. Flattered, we would laugh before I would go into why I was there before it happened.

On my third visit, I asked Misty how she was doing. She told me, "I ain't no damn Misty" and "I can't stand that bitch." I asked her that if she wasn't Misty, who was she? She told me her name was Karen and if I wanted to continue talking to her, don't bring that punk bitch Misty name up to her. Karen told me "if Misty had listened to her rather than them other motherfuckers they wouldn't be where they are right now."

To say I had never seen anything like this before would be the truth. I told Misty to stop fucking with me and that I had driven a long way to see her. Karen cursed at me and reminded me that she wasn't no damn Misty. This time, I believed her. When it hit me, I sat there and she asked me why I looked like I wanted to cry? I told her I did. Without asking me why, she said fuck Misty. Not knowing what to do, I just sat there in silence for about an hour. The guard came in to check on us, Karen asked to return to population and she left.

On the drive back to Atlanta, I asked myself, what happened to my little girl. How long has Misty been a schizophrenic and when was she first diagnosed. Did her trial and appellant attorneys know of her condition? I had so many unanswered questions and so many concerns. Hurt and confused, I wept driving back to Atlanta.

When I got back, I called Misty's father for money to have an independent psychiatric evaluation done. I had a friend and colleague that specialized in representing people with mental illness. In Atlanta in the mid-nineties, clients that suffered from mental health issues were a non-concern in the criminal justice system. Thus, even if I were to show that Misty was suffering from a mental illness, she was not guaranteed a new trial. However, it was an angle and it wasn't going to hurt anybody to try.

Doctors and social workers descended on Misty and evaluated her for a period of weeks and prepared a report for me. Doctors believed that Misty had been molested by her father. The report mentioned that the reverend was not only physically abusive to Misty but also to her mother. Moreover, that Misty had been molested by her uncle for years and actually grieved for him when he died.

The report found it odd that Misty still cared for him. And sadly, I had not met all of Misty's personalities. To me, Misty being molested by older men was nothing more than Misty seeking the love she wanted from her father. For Misty, a younger man could not fill the void she needed to sustain her. For her molesters, older men can sniff out young pussy looking for a daddy like an old mangy dog can sniff out food. Thus, the older men sensed Misty's needs and over time repeatedly abused her.

With the report in my hand, I met with Misty to go over the information in the report. It was really a wasted trip, by the time I got to the prison, they had given her so many drugs that she couldn't keep her mouth closed, and the drool just went from her mouth to her lap and then to the floor. I attempted to talk to Misty anyway. I had missed her. Misty didn't know of any Karen, when I asked how she was doing. She called the evaluators nasty for suggesting that she'd been molested by her dad. Misty refused to talk with me about her uncle. Seemingly, she still had love for him and that was hers to keep. With the interview not going anywhere because of her condition, I returned to Atlanta.

Misty's dad called me outraged at the notion that he had slept with his daughter. The fact that he had paid these people to help Misty, he felt betrayed by them. He never mentioned anything about his brother messing with her. I wondered was his silence cowardice or just something he couldn't do anything about since his brother was dead.

Months went by, before I was able to make the drive to Misty. Her dad had reported me to the State Bar claiming I hadn't done shit on her case and he wanted his money back. In my mind, he was shitty with me for the report the social workers had completed. He was now aware that I was looking at his ass with the left eye of suspicion to see if he were the bully the report said he was. I told the State Bar that I wasn't giving him shit back. In fact, if the minister refused to pay me an additional dime, I would continue to correct the injustice brought against Misty pro bono. The State Bar sided with me but lit a fire underneath me to wrap it up and gave me a time line.

The next time I visited with Misty, she had tattooed some woman's name to her neck. I asked Misty whose name she had branded herself, when I was told that Misty wasn't present. I was told that I was talking to Helen and she didn't know where Misty was and she tried to avoid Karen's lesbian ass when she could. Helen didn't know about any of this social work stuff or Misty's father reporting me to the State Bar. However, she had heard Misty talk about me.

I asked Helen what did Misty say? Helen said that Misty had told her this stuff in confidence and she shouldn't tell me. I essentially begged Helen to tell me what Misty had said and she finally did. Helen told me that if I didn't get Misty a new trial it didn't matter no way, she wasn't going to live the rest of her life in here. I told Helen to tell Misty that the writ of habeas corpus was done and I just needed her to sign this document for me. I told Helen that I had come today for Misty's signature and would she be kind enough to sign it for Misty to save me another trip and she did.

When I left Misty, I went straight to the Courthouse and filed Misty documents and got a court date. I was excited. I was able to line up a psychologist and Misty's prior attorneys to testify on her behalf. It was all set, when I got a visit from the minister, Misty's dad. He told me that he wanted me to dismiss the habeas. I was confused. He had reported me for not getting the thing done and now he wants me to withdraw it. He told me that I needed to accept the fact that Misty was ill. He told me that he and his wife could not take care of her in the way she needed care. More, importantly, they feared that if Misty were released, she would be hurt, end up dead or hurt another and they couldn't live with that.

I told the minister that we could try to get her committed to a hospital. He asked me if I could guarantee that the court would do that. I told him I could not. The minister did not want to get Misty's hopes up again only to disappoint her in the end. I asked him where was his faith? He said with God. He told me that he had prayed on the matter. The minister then asked me if I had any kids. I told him that I did not. He looked at me as if my answer confirmed his decision, me being childless couldn't possibly understand the decisions he had to make for his own. The minister told me to stand down.

I knew that Misty had been into several fights while in prison. I typically never concerned myself with one's propensity to commit future crimes. However, if she were released, I wouldn't want anything to happen to Misty. I would feel responsible if something did. And in-spite of everything, I knew her father loved her more than I ever could.

The moral ambiguity of life decisions that some have to make is to be understood only by them. The moral confusion in my own life, I have to learn to figure out and live with them. Misty is still incarcerated and has served over seventeen years of a life sentence. I'm so sorry Misty. Please forgive me, your friend.

THE CITADEL

For all he could have been, he would never be. For all she had sacrificed for him, she lost. He had crushed her dreams, the life she had planned for him. She still loved him enough to come see me. In an awkward sort of way, she wanted me to love him. She wanted me to care. Unbeknownst to her, I did care, but not for the reasons she wanted. A mother's love for her son takes on so many different meanings. History has shown us that a woman who bore a son as a first-born solidified her retirement by adding status to that queen's life. In an instant, she's now becomes mother to the heir of the throne. Likewise, it was no secret to my sisters that my mother had a special love for her boys.

At the time, Raymond was the only person I had met that graduated from the prestigious Citadel. Established in 1842, prior to the civil war, it was the only institution in the south that rivaled WestPoint in upstate New York. On paper one could be impressed with the fact that Raymond had done it. He graduated. To have attended such a school that specialized in building character and integrity in tomorrow's leaders, Raymond was expected to be special. At least, that's what his momma figured. Little did she know, Raymond just wanted to pretend to be a Nigga. Everybody knows that Niggas don't graduate from The Citadel.

I recalled how she looked at me doing the trial. She had given me the impression that she was an elitist, pleased with her choice of counsel. She had found herself Mr. Charlie and she was content. She even frowned at me as I argued a point on behalf of my client Red. I sensed some condescension in her glare at me, as if she was afraid to look me in the eye. Of course, I forced her to speak. "Good morning," I said. She replied the same. Then, I could detect her Caribbean accent in her voice.

I had heard discussions that other black folks of the world viewed African Americans as soft and spoiled. Rightfully, they understood that a number of African Americans became system people or tried real hard to obtain that status. Hence, why work when you can get shit for free. Foreigners, understood that African Americans had lost their identity somewhere after Jim Crow and Affirmative Action; a time when the government put black women in charge over black men.

Today, the African American community is as fractured as during the time of slavery. I guess foreigners recognize these broken communities and learn to profit off their needs. Thus, we see a collection of Chinese Soul Food places and Indian convenience stores, wherever blacks can be found. On the contrary, seldom do we see black owned businesses in their communities. I guess Raymond's mother smugness toward me had some reason if not validity. To the contrary, she had me wrong.

If she had known that I literally told Mr. Charlie to separate Raymond's trial from Red's, it could have changed things. I told Mr. Charlie that I was going to point the finger of guilt at Raymond before the trial started. I did this as a professional courtesy. But, Mr. Charlie didn't know me and to take heed to the inside information was beneath him. He was Mr. Charlie.

When the trial started and as promised the finger pointing began. At a recess, Mr. Charlie rushed into my space, put his finger in my chest and demanded that I meet him in the hall. Before, I realized it, I told Mr. Charlie, if he ever touched me again, I would fuck him up. I told him to lower his fucking voice when he addressed me.

Before, he could apologize, I told him from now on address me as "Mr. Johnson." Yeah, I had a "Mr. Tibbs" moment and I meant it. Conceivably, Mr. Charlie could have reacted the same way to anyone doing what I had done to his client. To the contrary, to this day, some of my friends refuse to drive a Mercedes or any German car for that matter. Likewise, given the shit that I've been through, I'm the same way with some exceptions.

I recalled going to my friend and law partner's bachelor's party at Lake Tahoe. Even though, I don't golf, this was my friend and he really wanted me there. After a day on the links, we went to a bar for drinks. My partner's law clerk got intoxicated and patted me on my head. It took the restraint of "God" for me not to fuck him up right there and spoil my friend's party. Seemingly, the whole bar got quiet and waited on my reaction.

I felt responsible that my friend have a good time at his party. Although, it would not have been my first bar fight, I didn't want to tarnish the occasion with this shit. So, I swallowed the humiliation. My friend understood that his clerk fucked up and needed to stay clear from me, when we returned to Atlanta. His apology was as empty as his conduct was racist. At the wedding in the heart of South Carolina, my friend's wife thanked me for keeping my cool. Although, I felt victimized and I was, it wasn't about me, it was about my friend.

After witnessing my aggressive behavior toward Mr. Charlie, the old judge threatened to hold me in contempt and put me in jail. Ain't that a bitch, Mr. Charlie stepped to me all crazy, but I'm the one threatened with jail. Like in basketball, it's always the second foul that gets called. The judge dared me using such language in his courtroom. He called me into his chambers and essentially told me, I would not have tried that in front of a white judge.

Three years later, Raymond's mother is sitting in my office asking me to help her son. I had gotten Red off. Perhaps, I could get her son a new trial. She had come to my office with a friend. I was patient with her and I sincerely tried to understand what she's been through. But, Raymond wanted to be a Nigga and he got what Nigga's deserve when they kill someone.

Raymond had only been home a month or two after graduation. His friends, who appeared to be many, were not college grads, none had jobs and my client Red was a little dope boy from Mississippi that Raymond met through a friend.

Raymond was dating this pretty little chocolate drop, with this long mane of crinkly hair. She stood about 5'6', with heals and sported a beautiful smile. She knew she was hot, a looker, but she dressed the part anyway; tight jeans; halter top, spiked heels. If she were in your presence, you were going to look.

Raymond took her to the corner store. The guys hanging outside of the store began to do what simple ass men do, comment on her ass, tits and things. Raymond felt that he was disrespected by the comments. He returned home and told his friends. Raymond and friends armed themselves and returned to the store. Raymond yelled out as he smashed a windshield of a car with the butt of a gun, "what now!" The natives scattered from the store before shots rang out. There was no evidence that the men that hung out at the store had guns or threatened violence against Raymond and his crew.

In the melee, an innocent by-stander was gunned down and killed as he exited from the city bus. Police determined that Raymond had a small army with him of about ten guys, Red being the outsider. At trial, it was easy for me to just point the finger away from Red since this was by all accounts Raymond's mess. The jury agreed and let Red go, not guilty on all counts. The victim was shot with an assault rifle and it was clear that Raymond only had a handgun, but I didn't care, it was still his mess, so he should have to clean it up. Notwithstanding, that Raymond's friends all put the assault rifle in Red's hands. I smugly told the jury they were just lying for Raymond.

I didn't know what to tell Raymond's broken mother. She was quite humble to me this time around. I understood it must have taken a lot for her to call and come see me, but she did. I refused to take her money as she attempted to give me a consultation fee. The power of love is unabiding and like a river, it seeks its own level. Sadly, I couldn't help her but I did tell her that I told Mr. Charlie what I was going to do. Years later, I returned to that county where Raymond was tried. As I stepped in the courtroom, I heard someone call my name, "Mr. Johnson!" It was Mr. Charlie. He was now a judge. He said to me, "Are you sure you want me to hear your case?" I smile and said, "I'm sure I don't." Mr. Charlie applauded my decision. He called me a good lawyer.

Sentence: *Life in prison*

JUSTICE

*"Men acquire a particular quality by constantly acting a
particular way...You become just by performing just acts."*
Aristotle

A friend of mine told me that sometimes he finds that integrity is on a sliding scale and its okay. But, for some they chose the path of the self-righteous which makes them a hypocrite. Although, what he said to me at the time sounded profound, I thought it to be a bunch of bullshit. I sat quietly so that my learned District Attorney friend would dismiss my case. His point was that some lawyers evaluate cases based on whether they thought they could win as opposed to the guilt or innocence of the matter. He opined that it didn't make the prosecutor a bad person if she decided to pursue a case that was otherwise weak or sounded funny, if not just incredible. Besides, doing your best doesn't amount to shit if you don't win.

The more I thought about what he said, the more it infuriated me. I knew if the matter involved someone he loved, the matter would not be just a competitive exercise for him it would be personal. As I sat approvingly of this bullshit, my attitude was that either the one charged with deciphering guilt or innocence will dutifully carry out that duty as a person of integrity and fairness or you were no better than the asshole that committed the crime.

I thought either you were going to do what is morally right or you were worse than the down low brother that no one really knows. You represent one thing but inside you're something dark and dangerous.

At least, we all knew who Hitler was. To accept integrity on a sliding scale speaks to one's lack of reliability and consistency. I take great pride in doing what I said I was going to do. Even, more, my friends and family expect me to.

Don't get me wrong, I've played the dependency game for a long time and now it has become a habit. Yes, I've encouraged people to believe and depend on me for my own selfish reasons. Turns out, this self serving game has become one of the few good habits I have. I clearly understand the sport of crime and punishment. In fact, I'm guilty of playing the game from time to time. Just like the little boy that beats his drums in the crowded apartment building to every ones displeasure. He doesn't get better if he doesn't practice.

At some point, we hope the question of morality gets stuck in a lawyer's head. One hopes that the lawyer's morality doesn't dissipate with the fee she receives for taking a case. Just like a woman that accepts a gift from a man that in heart she knows she doesn't deserve, but in the moment she is better off having taken it. The proverbial gift with strings attacked. Inevitably, she regrets the fallout on the back end. Although, she knew in the beginning it's never really a clean break. Like most men, she knows that he will expect some sympathy, breakup or obligatory pussy that he feels he's entitled to. Not that she'll eventually give in; it's just the laborious process of telling him no that gets old.

Regretfully, I have lived under this false premise of professional necessity at the expense of others and making myself whole. Unlike a lynch man or Nazi, whom claimed that they were just following orders. I'm guilty of doing shit for the money, but I've never had to kill anybody. When does this reckless attitude end? Well it can stop for me, when those responsible for crime and punishment take their integrity off of that imaginary sliding scale and consistently do the right thing. Thus, when they stop, perhaps I will stop, but until then I'll do what I have to do.

Until then, I will not balance the mayhem that my client is accused of against the interest of those that loved the decedent. Instead, I will continue to sing the same old songs "he killed the man but he's not that bad of a person" or" he killed a man because he deserved killing," which was the case of Clarence Thomas.

Clarence Thomas was a man in his late fifties early sixties, but he looked eighty years old. A hard charging life of alcohol and chasing younger women was a life that had a high cost and took its toll on Mr. Thomas. I met Mr. Thomas at the Fulton County Hospital. Judge Deneaux asked me to represent him and that she would pay me with county funds. I agreed. At the time, Mr. Thomas was suffering from kidney failure along with cirrhosis of the liver from a life of partying. When I entered his room, there was a younger woman there half his age tending to him. I felt she was actually younger than me and I was in my mid thirties.

I first introduced myself to Mr. Thomas and then to his younger lady. I know I looked at her as a gold digger shoveling for Mr. Thomas' disability or retirement check. She looked right back at me like if I wanted, she'd take a little of my change to because it was business for her. I wasn't there too long before she kissed him and left. Shortly after she was gone, I asked Mr. Thomas what in the hell before he snapped at me, "the hell with being by himself."

Mr. Thomas lived in subsidized housing and just needed a little money for food and whatever. He didn't mind paying for company. I laughed out loud and called Mr. Thomas a freak. Mr. Thomas asked me if I were married. I told him that I was not. He told me if he had my life he wouldn't need to buy shit either. I allowed him to make assumptions about me. We were bonding. When Mr. Thomas asked me if he could offer me some advice; I said sure. He told me "to keep living."

Mr. Thomas was accused of killing a teenager with a shotgun after the boy attempted to break into his home. Mr. Thomas told me that he had warned those boys time and time again, to stop selling that shit in front of his house. Not one to call the police, Mr. Thomas only threatened that he would and in the past, the threat worked.

One afternoon, the boys posted up and started selling that shit again and this time his threat didn't scare them off. The boys had ripped the phones cords from the box outside of his home. At the time, Mr. Thomas did not own a cell phone and people were still walking around with pagers attached to their sides. Mr. Thomas told me that he went to his front door which was secured by a metal screen door and burglar bars. He opened the door but left the outer screen door locked. "I told ya'll to stop selling that shit in front of my house." One of the teens said fuck you old man and the group began to laugh. When Mr. Thomas made the same announcement, one of the teens approached his door and attempted to break it down.

Mr. Thomas left the door for a few moments and returned with his shotgun. He told me that he told the teen to get away from his door. The teen refused and continued his efforts to break into Mr. Thomas' home. As he picked up the phone to call 911, the phone was dead and Mr. Thomas returned to the door. He told the boy, "don't come in here, I'm gon shoot you." The teen continued and Mr. Thomas fired a warning shot into his ceiling. This made the boy try even harder to enter Mr. Thomas' home. The boy began to threaten Mr. Thomas. The boy told Mr. Thomas that he was going to kick his old ass once he got inside. Mr. Thomas said it was a damn shame because he's the one with the gun, but he was still afraid. Boom! The teen was fatally shot through the metal screen door.

I asked Mr. Thomas, if he saw the boy with a gun. He told me that he thought he had one because the boy kept coming. I asked him if he had seen a gun. Mr. Thomas said honestly, he didn't wait to see. He feared for his life when that fool kept trying to come in his home. Mr. Thomas said it was crazy for them to charge him with first degree murder when he only tried to defend himself. I agreed. I knew that my song for this case was the teen deserved killing.

Mr. Thomas eventually got a little better and was released from the hospital. I was able to get Mr. Thomas released from jail on his own recognizance. I asked the judge where would he flee to dialysis? Once I got Mr. Thomas out of jail, he would come to visit me from time to time and we would talk about his case. Sadly, he would call me from the hospital more than he would come to the office. On one occasion, Mr. Thomas wanted me to prepare a power of attorney for his only surviving relative, his brother that lived somewhere in Ohio. I did and took it up to his room for him to sign.

Hot damn! Mr. Thomas had a different woman in the room rubbing his forehead with a towel. We made eye contact and smiled at the moment we just shared. He asked her, "Baby step out for a second." I told him Mr. Thomas, "You're something else." Again, he told me to keep living. I said this one is younger than the other. He said a rabbit with one hole is a poor rabbit before we laughed again. I asked Mr. Thomas, "what you trying to do get more pussy than me." He looked me up and down before he said that was impossible with all these young heifers in Atlanta. Besides, he said, his little change couldn't compare to my check, and "I ain't had no pussy in a long time." I noticed all the tubes coming from his body. I said "you just wanted me to see what you got in the stable." Quietly, he gave me a Fred Sanford dirty old man smile and I smiled with him.

As we began to talk about his case, Mr. Thomas told me he didn't want to die in prison. The mood became somber and reflective. I told him that he wouldn't because his case was some bullshit. Mr. Thomas kept saying he didn't want to shoot that baby and began to cry. Of all the people I've sat with accused of murder, I can never counsel them on their soul. I just tried to console him on how he would not spend the rest of his life in prison. I imagined that Mr. Thomas had a lot to cry about with his medical situation staring him in the face and the stress of this shit. He was tired. Months later he died.

However, it wouldn't be fair for me to take out my sliding scale of indifference and accuse the state of Mr. Thomas' murder. You know, sue the state just for kicks because I think I can win or at minimum milk the situation for free publicity. This teen ripped the telephone cords out the box and was attempting to break into Mr. Thomas' home. Because Mr. Thomas can't prove that the teen had a gun, he's charged with murder and facing life in prison. Really, and you call me a self-righteous hypocrite even if I think I can win?

MEASURE

*"Some People would rather see you
die than to see you fly..."*
Sean Combs

J ake was an easy going man, "the help your neighbor type." At least that's what his neighbors black and white told the jury. Anyway, I had no reason to doubt them. At first, I did feel some shame when I was obsessed with the thought of accusing Jake for his own death. It didn't matter to me that he was killed in his own house or killed by someone he loved. I even thought him to be a homosexual, which I couldn't prove and I only had evidence to the contrary. Still, I knew his sexuality had nothing to do with anything nor could I measure his death with my simple minded and convenient homophobia. Whatever, he was during in his life I knew he was better than most folks I had met.

I mean, he wasn't perfect. His friends told of his selflessness, idiosyncrasies and his hermit like habits, but even this did not make him weird. I don't like a lot of folks in my space let alone in my house. Some people like to entertain and some like to be entertained, and I fall in that group. Folks that need to be around a lot of folks are no more balanced than those of us who don't. Comparing myself to Jake, I find that the older I get, I become increasingly private. Hence, I found that Jake and I had something in common.

Retired, Jake was working at a tire shop to have something to do. He was not the type to sit at home and bask in his retirement. From West Virginia, all Jake knew was how to work. Single and no kids, Jake's friends were his family. Especially, the fellow West Virginians that moved to Georgia with the promise of jobs after the plant closed. It came out, that Jake dated Tillman's mother, Pamela Rose before he was born up until Tillman was about thirteen years old. Jake was even in the hospital when Tillman came in to the world. However, Jake was not Tillman's father. Known as Pam to her friends, Pam was in her thirties and from Alabama. Pam had met Jake shortly after she moved to Atlanta. A southern beauty schooled in the latest fashions of decorum, manners and style. Pam was fine.

As with a number of Southerners, Pam would speak slowly and in a calm tone that gave her conversation a certain rhythm and air of politeness. She spoke with a certain intimacy that was sincere. A sincerity that kept your attention as she explained herself. Tall, yet very curvaceous, Pam would do any man proud and she knew it. Jake being nearly fifteen years her senior felt dignified to be of importance to her. Besides, Jake didn't mind paying for shit unlike men of Pam's generation. Jake was born in the late 1940's or early 1950's, nearly the last generation of men that were taught chivalry.

The only knock on Pam that I sensed was her passive aggressive nature. When you coupled the polite tone of her conversation with her suggestive demands, one could get confused with her signals. Likewise, when folks can't tell you what they really want out of moral pretense, it can get frustrating. For it was beneath Pam to just come out and tell you what the hell she wanted. In this game of mental charades, Pam needed you to figure it out. She needed proof that you were really paying attention and you honestly cared.

I don't know if Pam was in fact high maintenance, she just appeared to be. I know it's hard for me to figure shit out even though in the past I've found myself trying to anticipate another's needs. Seemingly, when you get it right, its gravy, but if you don't, you get accused of not paying attention or being selfish. Even worse, you just can't get shit right because you're just a fuckup. One thing Pam did make abundantly clear was that she would do anything for her son and she wanted me to get him off.

Pam told me how she had reared Tillman in the church and how her girlfriends were his Godmothers. A single parent, Pam told me stories of how she scraped and borrowed to send Tillman to private schools. She was grateful that when she would fall financially short, Jake was there with a check. A willing giver, it was inevitable that they would date. Love has always been a learned behavior if you have any sense of gratitude.

In fact, you could learn to be in love with the idea of love if you been in enough fucked up relationships that I've been in. The cliché of help them that help you can sincerely turn into love over time and have real meaning. Thus, shaking off the cheap reference that some like Pam had given to us as the help. Pam loved Jake. To me, Pam's love for Jake epitomized what my mother told me as a child, "You'll love the first time for the sake of love. The next time it will be for other reasons." Jake was good to Pam and Tillman.

Pam had referred to Jake as Tillman's Godfather on several occasions. I let her get away with it. I knew she had to warm up to me before she confessed. I respected her privacy. However, I knew she had fucked Jake well before she told me. At first, I thought Pam referring to Jake as a Godfather was the new thing. When I was a kid, it was my friends that had an Uncle Buck that they couldn't explain how he was related. Nor could they explain, why he was allowed to go in their momma's bedroom when Uncle Ralph never went beyond the kitchen.

Pam eventually married another man and Jake took it quite hard. I don't care how gracious a man tries to be, it hurts when another man is sleeping in the bed he bought and enjoying the comforts that he provided. In Pam's mind, she tried to hang in there with Jake, but other than buying shit, Pam was a younger woman that had needs. Not one to fuck around, she told Jake of the much younger man. In fact, this one was younger than Pam. Pam realized she was emotionally hungry.

I don't think this made Pam a bad person any more than it made Jake look silly thinking Pam was going to starve forever. I mean a hungry person will find food at some point even if they have to steal it. Jake just found himself faced with the inevitable dilemma of the younger pussy and the older man syndrome. Jake wanted to play and Pam gave it a shot. It wasn't meant to last forever, measure what you've enjoyed. Dream about the measure you're missing and try to enjoy that. Personally, I don't think it made them bad people to have played a little. But, I can't talk. I've been guilty of holding on to shit much too long and after spending a few dollars holding grudges, when shit didn't go my way.

Tillman and three friends drove seventy-five miles to Macon from Atlanta. They had planned to just burglarize Jake's home, perhaps steal the safe that Tillman knew he kept in his basement closet and leave. They didn't expect Jake to be home, but he was. Jake told a friend that he had to get off the phone because his Godson was at the door. He promised the caller that he would call her back, it was the last time she would hear his voice.

After Tillman was allowed in the house, he summoned his friends Jason and Bullet. Becky the driver stayed in the car. The three took Jake to his bedroom at gunpoint and rummaged through his stuff. As Tillman made eye contact with Jake, I imagined that Tillman began to stare at his framed baby picture still resting on Jake's nightstand as Jake stared at him. Jake's eyes were filled with love, confusion and disappointment as his heart is now consumed with betrayal by the boy he loved as a son.

Not finding what they were looking for, Tillman directed Jake to the basement where the safe was found. After Jake opened the safe, he was placed on his knees and shot in the back of the head execution style. I wondered why Jake chose not to fight for his life. I wondered if I could chose love over death when death came knocking on my door. If I had it in me to kill my son if he tried to kill me or would I let him live like Jake chose life for Tillman. I love my son and because of my love, I would give my life and perhaps kill for my son. However, I would not let him take my life. I am not Jesus nor was Jake.

After calls to Jake's phone went unanswered and he failed to report to work or call in, his friends and co-workers called police. Jake's body was found two days later and the investigation began. Jake's neighbors and friends were sure about one thing and that was that Jake did not allow many people inside his home. Thus, with no sign of forced entry, Jake must have known the person that killed him. Police checked Jake's cell phone records and found the last call was to his friend. Police contacted the friend, who told police about Jake's beloved Godson's visit. Police wanted to talk to Tillman.

When I first met Tillman, I thought of him as a beautiful looking athlete, 6'6", teenage skinny, with broad shoulders, a basketball coach's dream. But, instead we're here in this musty room discussing how it came about that Jake was killed and he was possibly the last person to see him alive. Shackled from his waist, hands and feet, Tillman was forced to shuffle from side to side because the shackles made it nearly impossible for him to walk. As I questioned Tillman, he whispered as he talked. At first I thought him to be afraid and shy, which was not unusual for the circumstances. But, after a while, I'm convinced that his demeanor was reserved in order to check me out. It took nearly a year before the case was called to trial. As it turned out, Tillman's case had been separated from the others. I guess no one wanted to sit with us. Tillman was the only connection to Jake, not them. I thought it was a smart strategy and very gracious of the judge to have allowed it. I guess we all knew if these kids had been just a few years older, we would be talking about a shot in the arm with the death penalty juice.

At trial, I begged the judge to throw out Tillman's confession because the police didn't allow him to talk to his momma before he confessed to his role in Jake's murder. I argued that the police conduct violated Tillman's right to an attorney. The judge agreed. Thereafter, I acted as if I knew Tillman was as innocent as Mother

Theresa pretending with all of my might that I didn't know he had already confessed. Deep down inside I knew, as with most trials there will be some shit that you just can't explain. And, the shit I had to deal with smelled worst than uncooked chittlins that needed cleaning.

I couldn't explain after Jake's murder, why a habitually broke Tillman was walking around his school with thousands of dollars and ounces of weed in his pocket. I couldn't explain why he and his friends enjoyed chicken wings and pizza they had bought with Jake's money as they watched a Monday Night football game. I couldn't explain why the only female that participated in the murder, Becky, went and got her nails and hair done after they returned to Atlanta. I also could not explain why a good suburban Christian boy was running with teenage vagrants that now refused to sit with him on judgment day. The explanation the state gave was that they just didn't give a fuck about Jake's life and the one that should have cared the most didn't. Even though it was true, I couldn't go with that.

The state gave the other three offenders immunity which forced them to testify against Tillman or go to jail for contempt of court. Eighteen year old Becky, whom was subsequently arrested for bringing weed into the jail for her boyfriend Bullet, was the first to testify against Tillman. To say that she spilled the beans on Tillman was an understatement. She was given a deal for less than five years for her role as the driver. Police tried to make a big deal of the fact that she returned the unused portion of her share of the fourteen thousand to the police. I quipped, not until she was arrested. Thus, her conduct didn't count as an act of contrition, let alone remorse.

Essentially, I asked Betty what kind of little bitch was she to get her hair and nails done after she knew a man they visited had been murdered. Betty replied, "The kind that hangs out with Tillman," Ouch! It was clear that every time I tried to show how fucked up Betty was she was going to drag Tillman in it with her. Betty reminded me of my oldest sister, Martha. She was a pro at hitting you in your manhood leaving you with that freezer burned look on your face. No, I knew to leave Betty alone. I knew that she was a sociopath, a street girl that was smart enough to fuck with me if I fucked with her.

Thereafter, the eighteen year old Jason was called to the witness stand. Jason admitted that he was a dope boy. Jason told the jury that he and Tillman attended the same school and were friends. At the time he spoke to police, Jason essentially said that he was so hungry that he agreed with whatever police told him to say. It didn't help that his statement was tantamount to a confession just like Tillman's. But, at least the jury hadn't heard about Tillman's confession.

The only adult male that participated in the murder, Bullet, Betty's lover was called to the witness stand. Unlike, the others, Bullet invoked his Fifth Amendment right not to incriminate himself twenty three times and was found in contempt of court. He was sentenced to 2 years in jail for his refusal to testify. I don't think he cared, 2 years to serve in the County Jail doesn't compare to life in prison without parole upon a conviction for murder.

The state then called two teens as witnesses that had befriended Tillman and attended school with him. Both teens testified that Tillman did have a lot of money after he returned from Macon. They also confirmed that Tillman was hanging out with a bad crowd at the time Jake was killed and they all had traveled to Macon together. I asked them where they had gotten their information. They said Tillman. Even though I tried to blame Jake's murder on Bullet, the jury convicted Tillman of murder. The judge recessed the sentencing for me to provide information that will give her a reason not to sentence Tillman to life without the possibility of parole.

Months later, when we resumed, the prosecutor so eloquently argued that had Tillman not killed his Godfather, Jake would have been in court supporting him through this ordeal. She was right. During the robbery, Jake didn't put up any struggle. I imagined Jake just stared at Tillman as he did what he was told to do by Tillman and his friends. Ironically, Tillman robbed and murdered for something that was going to be given to him. Jake was saving the money taken by Tillman to buy him a car as a graduation present. Tillman was to have graduated from high school in a few months, when Jake was murdered.

Jake's older brother, a man of sixty-years or more told the judge that Tillman didn't give a damn about Jake and he was not the kid he had met, when Jake brought Tillman to West Virginia acting like a proud father. He was disgusted, if not outraged, to learn that Tillman ate chicken and pizza with Jake's money hours after they had killed Jake. He was hurt to learn that Tillman, as much as Jake loved him, left Jake's dead body to rot in the basement, where he had left him. He commented on how Tillman smirked during the trial as he sat at the defense table. Thus, Tillman showed no remorse for killing the man that loved him as a son. He asked the judge to sentence Tillman to prison for the rest of his natural life.

When it was my turn, I still felt limited by my circumstances since I could not discuss the schools Tillman had been kicked out of, which had been every school he had ever attended. The judge already knew even if the jury didn't that Tillman had confessed to his participation. Given Pam was a Christian lady with Christian friends, I decided to just have them speak for Tillman and they did. As expected, the Christians spoke of forgiveness. The Christians all spoke of the love they had for Jake. Moreover, they spoke of the love Jake had in his heart for Tillman. The Christians told the judge that they truly believed that Jake himself would have forgiven Tillman for what he had done.

Tillman's father told the judge that he had been estranged from Tillman most of his life. He told her that he was not a man that begs, but if it would help, he'd beg her not to sentence his son to prison for the remainder of his natural life. Shortly, thereafter, I asked Tillman's former step dad if Tillman had any redeeming qualities. He replied yes, before I asked him how did he know? He told the court that he'd hope that he had given Tillman his good qualities. He was sincere in his belief that his qualities were worth something and that the judge should believe that they were. I believed.

The judge recessed and took the matter under advisement for several hours. During that time, I broke my own rule. I asked Tillman, what the fuck? He had attended private Christian schools and was now a senior set to graduate. He had lived in the most prestigious communities in Atlanta and his Godparents were successful people that were active in his life. Tillman was not a kid that didn't know love. Unlike many kids, Tillman had a community of family and friends that provided a steady hand. So, I asked, what the fuck was he doing with these vagrants? I think the most honest thing Tillman said to me was that he didn't know why he was hanging with these people.

He had only known of these people for the duration of a semester in high school because he was a new student. I told him that there were a lot of people in my life that thought they were too good for me. Given some of the shit I used to do, they had every right to believe that and stay away from me. I told him you are better than people that don't want shit and its okay. Because, sometimes, it's just the way it is. Some people don't want shit and don't want you to want shit. Sadly, some people have forgotten how to dream. I guess you just were too young and blind to measure the life your mom had sacrificed and planned for you. As the judge returned from her recess, Tillman whispered in my ear that I was right. He couldn't measure the life that was his to live. Becky, Jason and Bullet were sentenced to serve 5, 10 and thirteen years respectively in the state penitentiary, as they accepted plea bargains to Voluntary Manslaughter.

Sentence: *Tillman life in prison with parole.*

MUSIC MAN

It was a typical Chicago winter, when it was so cold my black skin turned white and the streetlights provided imaginary heat.

Again, I found myself eating hairy ass chicken wings from Harold's Chicken quietly comparing them to my beloved Frenches' Creole Chicken in Houston, where it was still seventy degrees in December.

I would eat Harold's' with Doc because this is what he liked to eat and I wanted to learn. As we sat in his living room, Doc would tell me that he could eat chicken every day. He wasn't concerned with the stereotype that such a statement attached itself to since he was more of an intellectual than most and comfortable in his own skin. Doc had power.

Doc was tall but frumpy. He had a weak muscle in his left eye, which caused his eye to wander. However, he was not one of low self-esteem. In most cases, Doc knew his intellect was superior to yours, but not in a condescending way, however in a way that you knew just through conversation. I had wished to become a renaissance man too, cultured in the arts, music and well heeled even if I choose not to practice the etiquette. I wanted to become a man of sincere substance not just viewed as one.

So I would sit there and chew on those hairy ass greasy ass chicken wings and sip on Wild Turkey as Doc introduced me to Coltrane's

"Gentle Side" contrary to the syncopation and nuance of Miles and Clifford Brown, as if I were in school. We spent real time together in Doc's efforts to educate me and train my ears to the sound of improvised perfection.

He claimed that such was an oxymoron since the music changed each time it was performed. It was each Music Man's interpretation of what was inside them as they played. This interpretation made the music personal to the musician and the listener alike. Doc would then say the need for interpretation was essential for none of us could be what we were yesterday, so it was essential to catch the moment for we will never have it again.

At the time, I didn't think a country dude from the backwoods of Georgia could teach me anything that didn't involve servitude let alone culture, but he did. Doc changed my life forever. He introduced me to jazz. Doc and I would catch the acts running through Chicago at the Ambassador Hotel on Michigan Avenue. Doc's thing was to catch the legends before they leave. Farmer, Turetine and the new comers Doc felt had promise. Seemingly, these outing were like field trips to the laboratories of the masters.

As a good student, I wanted to learn from the man who worked as a Public Defender by day and an English Professor by night over at Roosevelt University. My wife had met Doc and his wife as they studied for the Illinois Bar Examine. We became fast friends since I was also new to town and had taken the bar a year prior.

I sat there and pretended to listen to Brad's mother as she described best she could all she had been through with Brad. How she had tried to love all her kids equally and give them life skills she thought they needed. She explained how Brad turn toward the worst after she had remarried. A proud woman, she began to cry.

As she cried, I recalled how Doc and I caught a young Roy Hardgrove at the Ambassador Hotel downtown Chicago. In the dimly lit cliché ballroom we sat on barstools that were elevated over the regular table and seats. Roy played for us with such melodic speed and intensity, he gasped aloud as he felt he slipped a note. Doc and I, along with fifty other people gasped with him. We all knew that Roy had us.

It was the first time that I understood what it meant to be spellbound. I had witnessed the sensation before, when I had taken a high school sweetheart, Rose to an Al Jarreau concert. We were in the 11th grade and it was a Thursday night, a school night. In 1979, a little known Al Jarreau was coming in to his own. As Al crooned, "I'm A Long Way From Home," and began to whistle, Rose drooled on herself. The drool ran from her mouth to her lap in a single but unified strand. I was impressed by both Jarreau's ability to make a woman drool and Rose's perfection.

Brad's mother was a petite lady, brown, simple eyeglasses with a girl next-door appeal. She wanted me to do everything I could to help him. But, at the same time she told me she was tired. She impressed upon me that she had always been there for him as to abort any judgment of her I may have had. I didn't tell her that I've heard it all before. I knew she just wanted some reassurance that I would help, if I could.

Brad had three open unrelated cases that escalated from a simple theft, to armed robbery to murder. At the time his crime spree began, Brad was only seventeen or eighteen years old. He had spent a life in the suburbs and good schools. He appeared to be bi-racial but I didn't ask. I knew from the looks of things, he was lucky enough to have known his mother's love, if he wanted. Also, I knew that he was about to live the rest of his life in regret, if convicted and sentenced to life in prison.

It takes awhile for young folks to realize or appreciate the consequences their acts have on others. Kids are blind to the ripple effect of the shit they set in motion. For them, the realization comes when they enter the prison system. Little Melvin out of Baltimore said that he realized it at that time. He said as he walked through the prison gates, "one guy wanted his shirt, the next guy wanted his shoes and the third guy wanted a kiss." Once this is experienced, reality sets in before the kid begins to cry, "Momma I want to come home, I'm sorry." Sadly, son it's too late now.

Brad was accused of killing an instructor of music, a Music Man that taught at Spelman College, the prestigious university for women in Atlanta Georgia. I can't think of any reason other than fate that the two would meet. The Music Man went into the bowels of one the worst communities in Atlanta to score some crack cocaine. He had lived in a seedy renovated hotel apartment in downtown Atlanta miles from where he was eventually killed.

Brad lived at least thirty miles away in a northern middle class suburb. I guess he was loitering and living as a runaway in Atlanta on the lamb from the pending armed robbery case in that county. Brad saw the gay, middle-aged thin white man as an easy target. After, the Music Man complained and demanded a refund for the fake drugs Brad had sold him. Brad shot and killed him.

There was no reason for Brad to have killed the Music Man because he was living with full-blown Aids and dying anyway. He just wanted to ease his pain as he lived out his life. Brad took it anyway. In the process, Brad forever changed the course of his life and those that loved him.

At trial, the case was assigned to the Honorable Diva Henry Williams Louis Mack. She was the first African American Chief Judge in the history of Atlanta. Hailed from the Southside of Chicago, she spoke with an English accent, which made me laugh. Diva disclosed that she would withdraw from Brad's case. Diva informed the attorneys and Brad that the Music Man had performed at her third marriage. Although, that marriage had dissolved and she was currently in marriage number four, Diva felt it necessary to disclose this fact.

I begged the Diva to stay on and that we waived any concerns of bias one-way or the other. I later explained to Brad that he was where he needed to be. At minimum, Diva would give him a fair trial. However, if convicted she too would give him a life sentence because she had to. Unlike, a few judges, they would not have given Brad any breaks and perhaps a life sentence without parole, if they legally could. Oh, contraire, he did deserve it.

Somehow, by the grace of God, I convinced the District Attorney to allow Brad to plead guilty to the reduced charge of Voluntary Manslaughter. Still, I knew along with the District Attorney and Judge Diva that Brad was about to become someone's bitch. A pretty bi-racial boy that was too skinny to protect himself, it was inevitable. In spite of the lost life of the victim, it's just hard not to have some empathy for Brad for his self-imposed tragedy.

In the end, the slender yet tall District Attorney showed me the Music Man's CD. She had worn a tight fitting brown business suit for trial that hugged her butt and contrasted nicely off of her beige skin. I noticed that the push up bra was working like it was supposed to. She looked clean and sharp. She was ready for trial. Excited, about the CD, I asked for a copy. She quickly said that she wasn't legally obligated to give it to me and she wasn't. I told her that it was for me. I explained to her how I loved music. After begging for a bit, she said that she would get me a copy but not today. However, the look in her eyes was that I didn't deserve it and she wasn't going to give me shit no matter how I flirted with her. I never got either.

But, that's okay, I know whatever happens, no matter how dire the circumstances, try as you might, you can't kill the music. For those that love music, it resides in your heart. For those that create music, it eternally dances in their soul. *"Rain drops on roses, whisker's on kittens, brown paper packages tied up with string,* the Music Man lives because music lives forever.

Sentence: *Twenty years to serve*

CHAPTER FIVE

FRIENDS

DEATH OF A BIRTHDAY
An Anniversary of Life

I know what it's like to want some pussy. Most men that love pussy do. So, when Tap called me and told me he had shot somebody about an hour ago and the police were looking for him. I didn't mind taking him to his girlfriend's house. I needed the time anyway to figure out how I was going to play his situation. I needed to figure out how I was going to play the angles.

As he went inside her apartment, I sat in my truck and puffed on a box of cloves cigarettes that Omar, my law partner had introduced me to. The clove is about the size of a cigarette but more hypnotic than a cigar. The sensation is not as mind altering as a joint. However, a novice like me didn't need much to get a buzz. So, I puffed because I'm not a smoker and never really learned the process of inhaling. For two hours, I sat in my truck and experimented with smoking cloves as I thought about how to play the angles. How could I help Tap?

My ex-recreational partner, Cindy was now dating Tap's brother. She convinced Tap's family to retain me and I kicked her back a few dollars like I was supposed to. I guess I had done something right when we were together. I've always been one for selective jealousy if it was advantageous to me. However, my jealousy seemed to come second to me getting paid. Thus, I am a businessman first.

Tap was a kid of the streets. He stood 5'10", football shoulders with chocolate skin. Tap sported chiseled cheekbones, white teeth and otherwise Hollywood looks. You could tell that his life had been rough. I recalled him being fearless and reckless for what he had been accused of, but I liked him. I liked Tap because he was a decisive young man. Tap knew that he was in some serious trouble. He knew that he could possibly go to jail if not prison for a long time. Tap realizing his circumstances, didn't flee the state of Georgia or attempt to leave the country. Tap just wanted some pussy.

At nineteen years old, Tap was a man. Some would say, like most men, he thought with the wrong head. In a strange way I understood Tap. I know what it's like to just want some pussy. I know some people would think how in the hell can you think of pussy after you just killed someone. After, you just permanently took someone breath away. How can your dick even get hard after life kisses death and blood is on your hands? Seemingly, Tap was just the decisive young man I thought him to be. At nineteen, Tap had an adult ability to compartmentalize.

Tap and a not so famous Rapper showed up as uninvited guest at a birthday party. Guys in one ghetto always become pensive when guys from another ghetto crash the party and start fucking with what's considered their women. The same lame arguments you find with inter-racial dating. The birthday boy had cautioned his friends just to be cool and celebrate his day. However, they took exception of how Tap walked around touching and rubbing on every girl that walked his way. They said Tap was loud and disrespectful, the type of behavior that just brought out the worst of those who shared his mentality. However, the partygoers say that the Rapper was cool. He just enjoyed himself and tried to fit in with other partygoers.

Eventually, birthday boy's mom asked Tap to leave. Tap left but talked shit on his way out. However, Rapper remained at the party. Tap was shitty that he was put out of the party before he could tell Rapper what was up. Thereafter, Tap convinced himself that Rapper was in some sort of danger when he returned to the party with a shotgun. Tap walked up to a side door and screamed for the Rapper "I just want my cousin!" The partygoers observing Tap with a shotgun went for their guns. During the shootout, birthday boy's older brother Travis was shot and killed. He was in his mid to early twenties. Before Travis was killed, in an effort to protect his mother and brother, Travis fired his 9mm and was able to graze Tap in the leg.

At first, it saddened me to know that for the rest of his life, birthday boy will mourn Travis' death. However, I hope eventually that he learns to celebrate Travis' life. Enjoy Travis life so immensely that those that knew Travis would look forward to it every year. I hope that Travis death on his brother's birthday becomes what it should be, an anniversary of life.

When Tap returned to my truck, I noticed the snatch gravy he had on the front of his jeans to go along with that bullet defect in his pants leg. I assumed that Tap got right to the point with his girlfriend. I smiled to myself and took him to Grady Hospital's Emergency Room. Grady was close and the only place that would take you if you didn't have insurance. Tap never asked me to call his mom or anyone for that matter. So, I didn't ask if he wanted me to. It was just us. As a gay male nurse was treating Tap, I asked for the police. Seemingly, the nurse knew what I was doing. He gave Tap a shot of antibiotics and a painkiller, before he threw some alcohol on Tap's leg, as if to say, Nigga ain't nothing wrong with you.

Both, the nurse and I knew that by going to the ER complaining of a gunshot wound, they had to do something or at least make a report of the visit. Hence, I was setting up my self-defense claim. Police took Tap's blue jeans as evidence. The jeans had a small defect where the bullet had entered and grazed Tap's skin. I now have medical records for a diagnosis of a gunshot wound and evidence to back it up. I told Tap that with such evidence, I'd have him out on bond real soon.

Now it was well after midnight on Friday-Saturday morning, as we waited on the paddy wagon to transport Tap to the county jail. I stood near Tap as he lay on his back staring at the ceiling from his gurney. When he looked at me with his now glassy eyes, we figured that the time he spent with his girlfriend was well spent. In the moment, he's shot up with painkillers and I assumed he had been sucked and fucked. Tap was ready to go to jail. I was glad I lived near the hospital because now I'm sleepy and feeling rather frisky myself.

It took me awhile, but I got Tap out of jail on bond. As always, once I get my client out of jail, I'm in no hurry to do anything. I think I managed to keep Tap's case on hold for a couple of years or for as long as I could before it was called to trial. Prior to trial, I had secured Tap's blue jeans from the police evidence room to use as evidence for the trial. However, again, the case was continued for some reason and I was glad. Still, I could not convince Rapper to come testify even though he possibly paid my attorney's fees.

During this time, my law partner Odis had left me. Private practice had taken its toll on him and it became too expensive for him to share expenses with me. At one time, we were up to six lawyers and staff in an office suite of three square feet. We were beautiful, me, Odis, Dana, Shakura and Kline. We were all thirty something beautiful and smart. Now, it was just me, and my ego wanted me to hold on to all of this space. As I continued to default on my rent, the leasing agent had decided to shut me down. Thus, I had to move all of my shit out of this office before I have bigger problems of not having my clients' files. In the process of moving, I lost Tap's dirty blue jeans with the snatch gravy and bullet hole in them.

Knowing what I know, I didn't think it was a big deal. I'll just call the treating physician or the nurse who treated Tap's injury on the night in question. To the contrary, I thought wrong, people are visual beings and I not having Tap's jeans was a problem. Moreover, it didn't help when the male nurse essentially testified in a very gay tone "that thug wasn't shot he was grazed" cost Tap dearly.

FACES I HAVE SEEN - *A Memoir of Murder*

I could never get Rapper to come to court. I couldn't be too shitty with him. We all knew what it was, Tap got mad because he was thrown out of the party for acting crazy. Tap returned with a gun and shot the place up. Tap senselessly killed Travis on his brother's birthday and the jury convicted Tap of murder. Rapper went on to celebrate a career in music and movies. Years later, Rapper ended up doing a little federal time for gun running. Twelve years later, Tap's case was reversed on appeal. In 2011, with an Atlanta legend and celebrity attorney as his counsel, Tap was again convicted of Travis's murder.

Sentence: *Life in prison*

JUST COOL

I sat there in my office and watched Cedric pass the polygraph examination. Cedric was rather smug if not proud of himself and felt even less remorse for the murder he had been accused. I knew in the beginning that polygraph exams were not wholly accepted as reliable evidence because of people like Cedric. The polygrapher was a former FBI agent who knew his stuff. Even though Cedric passed the exam, I could tell the experienced agent knew that Cedric had beaten the machine. To the contrary, Cedric knew that beating the machine was cool. However, could he convince his friend, Peter from accusing him of murder.

Peter had been in the drug game for years. As a result of his lifestyle, Peter was involved in one way or another in several murder cases around Atlanta, but somehow managed to escape conviction and sometimes arrest. I had met Peter through his girlfriend, Karen the daughter of a court reporter whom I had tried cases with before. On one of those murderous occasions, Peter had gotten arrested and the court reporter sent Karen to me on Peter's behalf.

Karen and I never got to the point in our conversation where we discussed fees. I was enamored with her and she knew it. Sometimes the energy that is exchanged between complete strangers fills the void where words would otherwise go. We knew that if I were to represent Peter there would be a conflict of interest. Karen felt it best that she use another lawyer. I agreed, when she invited me to her salon in the West End area of Atlanta and I went.

Karen had this dark smooth skin and pearly white teeth that contrasted nicely with her hair and face. She wore her hair to her shoulders and it had a natural bounce to it that forced her to remove it from her face when she'd move her head in certain positions. Tall, slender, nice ass, Karen was the total package.

The only knock on Karen was that she was a dope girl. As with most dope girls, they get strung out on the money before they get hooked on the lifestyle. I mean, there are a number of people who would love to sport around in luxury cars, expensive clothes and shit with money to burn. Oh contraire, most people would not sell their souls to the devil to have these things? The dope girl does and ultimately that's what burns her soul.

When I walked into Karen's salon, she was there attending customers. I didn't see anything that was opulent about it but it was hers and she was proud. I knew that Peter had fronted her everything including the sports car parked outside. Like most men, I didn't have the money to compete with the likes of Peter. Like a spoiled child, it's all about money with the dope girls depending on how long they've been in the game.

I thought to myself after seeing Karen's set up, I was lucky she felt any of my energy at all. I stepped away from Karen as soon as I attempted to step to her. Before long, she was pregnant with Peter's baby and I began to detest Peter even more. Funny thing is Peter never knew I existed let alone longed for his soon to be baby momma. As it turns out, Karen was just one of many women impregnated by Peter during this time. Karen had become a casualty of the dope boy legacy. The legacy of fatherless children and those of incarcerated dads.

Cedric tried to tell me that he got caught up into this shit trying to help a friend out. A person he had long admired and enjoyed hanging out with. Like Cedric, I never knew until now that friendship and loyalty are independent concepts. One does not define the other. I told Cedric that I didn't have many friends because I got tired of the disappointments. My friends were usually an emotional relationship that became economically taxing for me. I mean, I could be a good friend, but where were those who could be a friend to me. People would say, don't define friendship by the exchange of money. I would say, stop asking and give me my shit back because I need it. In my case they rarely do.

I asked Cedric what made him feel that Peter was his friend. Cedric told me how they attended the same elementary school together. He had known Cedric all of his life and they were cool. I asked, "I understand that ya'll were cool but what made you friends." Cedric explained how they played football at the park together and as adults how they even hustled together. So, in Cedric's mind, their history and experiences together made them friends.

I understood where Cedric was coming from. In Cedric's mind, he thought that based on their history in life together, he and Peter were friends. To the contrary, in Peter's mind based on this same life history, he felt that he and Cedric were just cool. Apparently, Peter understood that there was a difference between being cool and being a friend. Historically speaking, black folks have always had a tendency to become overly familiar with one another based on their associations with each other. Thus, time together and shared experiences mean friendship. Sadly, it doesn't. People have engaged in shared experiences and associations for a life time and hate each other to the core.

I explained to Cedric my association with fellow attorney Walter Robinson. I told Cedric how Walter Robinson would take me to visitations of folks he knew. I reflected on how I would sit in an anonymous funeral home of an anonymous person. Seemingly, Walter convinces me to ride with him from funeral to funeral and I do under the promise of food and beer. It's not like I can't buy my own it's just the conversation and laughter that comes with it that makes the trip worth it. This time we were at a wake of the mother of a friend who went to high school with Walter over twenty years ago.

We got there rather late so no one was there but Walter and I. As we sat in the parlor, Walter was trying to tell me something. I had zoned him out. At the time all I could hear was the sound of the vacuum cleaner. The funeral home janitor had begun to prepare the place for the next day. It felt rather surreal for me as I watched him vacuum around the parlor and casket before he asked me to raise my feet up. I obliged but against Walter's wishes, I asked Walter if we could go and we left.

On the ride to the restaurant, I told Walter that was my last funeral home run. The emptiness of the funeral home and the exaggerated white powder contrasting on the dark skin of the dead lady's face reminded me of my loneliness and the loneliness I felt for the dead lady. The business as usual attitude of the funeral home employee just hurriedly wrapping up so he can go home and catch the end of the game was all too much for me. Besides, I didn't know these folks and my idea of a good time was not to randomly attend funerals of folks I didn't know. Walter tried to convince me otherwise that shit like this is what friends do for one another.

After a while, I told Walter that this was some morbid shit and we laughed about it. This funeral thing we would do became a running joke just like everything else we talked about and lived for. As if our reality was too much to deal with because it was. I told Walter, friends my ass, I rode along for the food and beer. We were cool and perhaps friends, but this was my last funeral home run.

By chance, Cedric while driving his momma's mini-van encountered Peter in Southwest Atlanta at a gas station. Cedric had not seen Peter in months if not years. Peter complained to Cedric that he had fronted Moonie with some dope and he hadn't paid up or returned the drugs he was given. Peter decided to teach Moonie a lesson. Hearing the story, Cedric volunteered to help.

Peter got into Cedric's mini-van. The two men then drove to another location where Peter picked up a gun and returned to the area, where they knew Moonie would frequent. Upon their return, Peter confronted Moonie about his money. Again, Moonie cried broke and refused to give Peter a little something on the debt. As the two drove off, a furious Peter somehow convinced Cedric to shoot Moonie. Cedric did, fatally striking Moonie in the head or chest area.

Peter and Cedric fled the scene. It didn't take long for police to have a description of the van and a partial tag number. The shooting occurred on an evening in April, the sun still bright and people enjoying the beautiful spring weather. Peter being no fool had Cedric to drop him off at one his dope houses and told Cedric to get rid of the gun. Cedric told Peter that he would first return home with his mommas' van and switch cars.

Unbeknownst to Cedric, Peter's dope house was within walking distance to the police precinct. Peter fearing the worse and not wanting to share the blame called his lawyer, who made an agreement with the police. If Peter provided information on the shooter, he would only be used as a witness as opposed to a suspect. Peter did just that. Peter even informed police that if they hurried, they could recover the murder weapon at Cedric's house. It didn't take long before Cedric was arrested at home and charged with murder.

The murder he committed for a friend he hadn't seen in months if not years. A murder committed because of a chance encounter at a gas station. With Peter as the state's star witness, the jury convicted Cedric of murder in less than five hours. Thus, decisions of life and death were made so easily in the name of friendship.

For what it's worth, Peter got caught up in another murder case that I was on. Unfortunately, the state also indicted Karen's fine ass for murder, who now has two babies with Peter. But, the state eventually let Karen go. However, this time, I'm sure Peter will remember me for the rest of his life. This time, I flipped my client, a friend of Peter's. This time my client became a witness for the state against Peter. Peter is now serving a life sentence for murder. I don't know about Cedric, but I chuckled to myself about the irony of all of this.

In the past, I had attended funerals for Walter's mother, mother in law and friends. So, when Melvin died, a friend of Walter's mother I refused to go. Melvin was a former client of mine, who had asked me to fuck him. When I told him no, Melvin said that he would settle for dinner then. Melvin was all but 6'4" tall easily in his fifties and about 190lbs. He played the piano from time to time at various churches Walter's mother would pastor. I wasn't afraid of Melvin now. I would have been as a homophobic young man in my twenties. I just found Melvin request of me to be funny. So, I laughed. I laughed so hard that I told Walter of Melvin's play on me and Walter told the world.

Some say that your friends will chose you to befriend but that doesn't mean you have to accept everybody's friendship. I would like to think that I have a friend or two in this world. Moreover, I want to believe that my friends would love me enough to help me if they could. I'd hope they would inconvenience themselves just a little to help me. I wouldn't ask anyone to kill for me, but if they did, I wouldn't tell on them. Likewise, if I did, I'd hope they wouldn't tell on me. In reviewing the list of folks I would consider friends, I reserve the right to revoke their friendship status. I'll just say like Peter, I'm cool with a number of folks. I'll hang on to that friendship thing to see what happens. Like Jesus, I know why that rooster keeps crowing.

Sentence: *Life*

FIVE O'CLOCK ON FRIDAY

I'm in a small town in middle Georgia seventy five miles south of Atlanta. The bell tolled every hour on the hour in the town square, which reminded me of an old movie. I was waiting on a verdict. My client, Herman was from upstate New York and had moved to Macon Georgia for a better life. At least that's what I told him to tell the jury. He was only twenty years old and accused of murder. His first lawyer had died of brain cancer and he fired the second attorney in a dispute over money before his parents hired me.

Herman and three friends were accused of killing a seventeen year old in a drive-by shooting simply because they felt disrespected. Well, in fact, they were but they brought that ass whipping on themselves. Jack and Herman were friends from upstate New York. They had worked together at Taco Bell when they were seventeen years old. Jack had family in the Macon area and had spent time there as a kid. At some point, Herman's mother had moved to Atlanta after she divorced his father. Herman's dad lived in Washington DC and owned his own business. Eventually, even Herman's maternal grandmother moved to Atlanta.

Herman having remained in New York was shot and left for dead in a dispute over a girlfriend. During his recovery, Jack paid him a visit and told him of his plans to return to Macon. Jack suggested that Herman consider doing the same. Within weeks, Herman took Jack up on the offer and moved to Atlanta and within days, Macon Georgia.

Jack's promise of a place to live and a job was an offer Herman could not refuse. Besides, outside of family, it's not like he knew anyone in Atlanta. After Herman moved to Macon, the promises Jack had made were realized when Herman moved in with Jack's sister, Tameka. Tameka and her live in boyfriend Blake got Herman on at the fast food restaurant where Blake was the assistant manager over the fries. Herman had been in Macon for only three weeks before he was working. Herman's proud mom gave him her second car to get to and from work conditioned on his promise to enroll in college. On the surface, things were looking up for Herman before the drive by shooting killed the seventeen year old Antwan Jenkins.

The week before the murder, Jack and his girlfriend's brother Jason took Herman with them to confront Antwan over a stolen car and gun. While sitting in Antwan's neighborhood, the trio met up with Romeo another friend of Jason's. Apparently the stolen SUV belonged to Romeo. Hours earlier, Romeo had given a crack head five rocks of cocaine in exchange for the use of the truck. However, the crack head reported the truck stolen when Romeo didn't return it as agreed. The gun inside the center console belonged to Jack.

The trio and Romeo encountered Antwan on the street when Jack demanded the return of the gun. Antwan then pimp slapped Romeo to the ground and commenced to stumping his ass. Romeo's head bounced off the concrete sidewalk like a ball; this according to Jason, who stood by and did nothing. At trial, I asked Romeo in the spirit of former Assistant District Attorney Nancy Grace "if it hurt" before he said, "no." I asked him "if he cried" and he replied, "yes because I was mad."

Nancy Grace would ask a victim to describe the pain and suffering they went through by the hands of a defendant. After the victim would give details of their crucifixion, Nancy Grace would ask them "did it hurt?" In my gallows humor, I found levity in the point she was making. However, I never heard a victim tell Nancy, hell yes it hurt. Even if they did, it would not have been funny.

During the melee, Antwan's cousin had taken another gun from Jack and began to pistol whip Jack about the face with it. Again, Jason who was 6'4"; 270 lbs stood by and did nothing. Herman said he stood by and just watched. He didn't know the guys Jack was fighting and he didn't know Romeo well enough to help. See, it was only the first time that Herman had ever seen Romeo in his life.

After someone threatened to call police, the fight ended. Thereafter, Jack, Romeo and Jason had either had their ass whipped and property taken and not returned. Herman said it was a long ride home as Jack was furious with him for not helping. Jack was also upset with Romeo for getting stumped in the ground. However, Jack said nothing to Jason's big ass, who sat there and did nothing. I guess he couldn't say too much since he was fucking Jason's sister. Less than a week later, Antwan was shot down in his neighborhood by someone driving a car that looked exactly like the one Herman's mom had given him.

A witness claimed that he observed the car just before the shooting occupied by three black males. Word of the murder traveled fast through the little town of Macon. Police had learned of the fight Antwan had days before with Romeo, Jack and Jason. No one knew Herman's name so they referred to him as the guy from New York. It wasn't long before Herman became the odd man out. Jack's sister kicked him out of her apartment. Her boyfriend Blake told police that he believed that Herman was involved in the shooting, but said nothing that would implicate Jack, his play brother in law.

After talking with Jason, Romeo went to police first claiming that he was mentally disabled and received social security benefits for his illness. Clearly, Romeo was seeking to trump whatever interest police had in him for Antwan's murder with his evidence of self-retardation. Police then questioned Jack and Jason. Initially they all lied and denied any involvement in Antwan's murder. Thereafter, one by one they provided police with information that led to Herman's arrest for Antwan's murder. One by one, all three agreed to testify against Herman at trial for a plea bargain. However, in their hearts they knew that Antwan was their mess and not Herman's.

When I first met Herman, I didn't like him. I told him that he was a fraud. As we prepared for trial, Herman hit me with a few bible verses as if he converted his life over to God. I knew he thought that his religious conversion would change my opinion of him but it didn't. I didn't find Herman sincere besides I catch this religious conversion shit all the time. It ain't nothing new to me. His parents were Howard University graduates, but Herman hung out with people that could barely say their name without you having to ask for it twice. I guess this made Herman feel a part of something or connected. If being shot and left for dead in New York wasn't enough to change Herman, he just needed to surround himself with some crazy ass thugs to make himself feel thug like.

His mother was petite, poised and attractive. She appeared to be a spiritual woman. She had a calm voice, stood 5'4" with a medium brown complexion. His father was handsome and very articulate in a way that was not condescending. He tried to express his confidence in me but at the same time prayed for my strength to carry his ill-mannered son through this bullshit. They appreciated me for telling Herman about his choice of friends. You could tell they had been saying the same thing well before I came into the picture.

Generation X, Y, Z, I don't know what bullshit they've bought into but it smells. This "me" attitude of self loathing and misplaced anger has turned itself inside out. Crime has now replaced the need for attention that they felt shorted on when mom and dad separated and eventually divorced. What a joke they have become in their pseudo self expression. Such behavior that merely imitates another fool, who overcame the same odds, but kept it together and now expresses himself through gangsta rap music.

Sadly, they think that they know about life, but they really don't know shit. They think that they've struggled, but they have had more than so many people in the world that had nothing. My contempt for them is only tempered with the hope that they travel more and realize their blessings, born in America. Thus, these baggy pants wearing mumbling Motherfuckers really don't have a clue about life or sacrifice. As a society, we can't afford the homicides that comes along with their eventual education that prison is where you're headed. If not, where you need to be since you can't walk around and act civilized with the rest of us.

It was a Friday and the jury has had the case since 10 a.m. that morning. Herman asked me how long I thought the jury would deliberate. I lied to him and told him that I didn't know. However, I knew that the jury would return a verdict by Five O'clock. At five o'clock on Friday, for many the eagle flies because it's payday and the beginning of the weekend. My crazy ass dad would tell my desperate mother that he lived for the weekend as he dressed to leave for the evening only to return the next morning. Daddy would take a wash in the sink because we didn't have a tub or shower; wet his fine thinning hair and slick it back with Vaseline. With much enthusiasm, he'd leave the house looking like a black man with white man's hair.

As I waited for my verdict, I walked around this old Southern courthouse. I saw that some of the court rooms were equipped with balconies. I can't describe the emotion I felt running through my veins to see this reminder of another time much like the ringing of the bell. I attempted to juxtapose this historic scene with the reason I was there before I chastised myself for the momentary disrespect. I figured the people that sat in that balcony were victims of history. Herman was merely a casualty of his inability to choose better friends.

As I waited, I had time to check out another trial. In that case, a 60 year old lawyer told the judge if a woman wore certain clothing at a certain time of night around a man, she was asking to have sexual intercourse. This was opposed to the rape allegation she had lodged against her girlfriend's brother. As I observed the ease and conviction of this lawyer's comments, I knew that he was the one who wanted me to drink out of the colored fountain. This was only an assumption of mine, but a very real one. The female judge told this old lawyer that the banality of his statement bordered on the offensive. To hear twenty first century thinking in this small town eased some of my apprehension. However, the old lawyer's client was acquitted of the rape. I guess this Bible belt Macon community is still not open to lesbian relationships.

I was as anxious and nervous as I always am of waiting on the jury to return its verdict. I had hoped that the jury bought my argument that it was Jack, Romeo and Jason that had the problem with Antwan and not Herman. Herman had allowed Jack to borrow his car to go to the store, even thought Herman's mother had forbade anyone from using the car. How could Herman tell Jack no, after all Jack had done for him? Instead of Jack going to the store, Jack did a drive-by shooting with Romeo and Jason in tow.

I knew five o'clock was drawing near. I found out the hard way that people are conditioned that five o'clock is quitting time. It matters not that one is accused of murder and facing life in prison. It matters not that Herman was only a month from being a teenager, with his life in their hands. What does matter is that people have shit to do on Friday that's more interesting than deliberating over another teen victim of teen street violence.

Scott was one of two attorneys that grew up in my neighborhood. He was fifteen years my senior. In the sixties, he had played high school basketball with my now deceased older brother Randy. His family lived down the street from my family. I last saw him in Indianapolis Indiana at the fortieth anniversary of the Southside picnic. Scott tapped me on my shoulders and told me that he had come to the picnic to see me. Scott tried to keep my undivided attention as I continued to fellowship with my fellow neighbors. I wasn't trying to be rude but I didn't make it back to Indianapolis as much as I used to, when I lived in Chicago. Distance had something to do with me going home, but the longer you're gone the easier it is to develop a new life where you are.

Scott told me, "Not to let this shit get to me." The practice of law had taken its toll on Scott. He was frail and seemed consumed. His once lean frame held together by his broad shoulders was once a symbol of his athleticism and strength. Today, he looked old and fragile, but sincere. In the midst of him telling me this advice, I continued to talk, greet and meet with my fellow neighborhood friends. Eventually, Scott was gone. I don't remember saying goodbye or when he left the park. Scott was just gone.

By the time I made it back to Atlanta, Scott had killed himself. I guess he didn't want his wife to suffer through his inevitable slow death from cancer. I knew that Scott had suffered in his practice of law. I wondered if it was the stress that led to his cancer or was it merely coincidence. Scott was trying to tell me the same thing that attorney Boris had told me when I moved to Atlanta, "Don't forget to get your dick sucked because this shit will kill you." Every day as I leave the house, this is advice I keep in the back of my mind.

As I sat there, I wondered if I had acknowledged Scott's advice, which allowed him to slip away. How many people did Scott serve such a personal message? Now its 4:45 p.m., the jury light is on. The judge comes out and the bailiff hands her a note. She announces to the courtroom that the jury has reached a verdict. The jury piles back into the courtroom. I'm looking for a sign. At least some eye contact from a juror. A vote of confidence but none of them will look at me.

The bailiff returned the little piece of paper to the foreperson, a Hispanic man. I remembered him, the business owner. I'm shocked because Macon is still so black and white, but here we have a Hispanic foreperson. He read the verdict form in his modified English accent, "We the jury finds the defendant Herman not guilty of murder and not guilty on all counts."

The judge excused the jury and then excused us, when Herman all but ran out of the courtroom hugging his mother and grandmother. His father was to my left patting me on the back crying tears of joy. As we stepped outside that old ancient musty courthouse, it was a sunny day, slightly humid but I think our sweat was that of anticipation of the verdict. From the sweet embrace of the motherly hugs, Herman finally looked up at me and made eye contact. He knew that I knew that he had gotten away with murder. At the same time, the bell tolled indicating that it was five o'clock and it was Friday. So we all left.

Its seventy five miles back to Atlanta. On my drive back, I recalled how Herman hugged me and promised me dinner. I told him to just invite me to his college graduation. I hope he goes. He'll need a buffer to explain in his job interview how he got away with murder. Seventy five boring miles ahead of me, I'm tired and stressed out, whom shall I call? I don't want to end up like Scott. If I called Lucy, she's going to want to borrow some money. Pam, her son's case is still pending. I better not mix the two. June complains too much, but she's so damn beautiful and smells so sweet. Fuck it. Hello, June, it's me! Hey you, don't you know them damn student loan people keep calling me and the damn brakes just went out on my car. Wait a minute, wait a minute, June I want to see you are you busy? June replied, well come on then and bring some Moscato, its Friday.

CLEAN HANDS

I don't think that Abdul aimed as much as he reacted to what he perceived as a threat to his life. POW! A shot to the neck stopped the threat from inside the car. Unbeknownst to Abdul and Haseem, Quarter had opened the back door to Haseem's car before he decided to rob them. So, when Quarter was shot, he fell to the ground between Haseem's car and the ground. Abdul and Haseem knew that they were fish in a bowl if they continued to sit in Haseem's car and wait for the return fire, so they bailed out and fled on foot through the strange neighborhood.

Momo saw the car rocking from side to side before he saw the red, orange and pink flash illuminating from within the car. Momo said that he didn't hang around to see who was shot. Instead, Momo called his lawyer and told him that during a visit to his law office, Momo had taken his gun. Momo told his lawyer that his gun was given to a friend to use, but the friend got shot and he needed to recover it. Momo told his lawyer that part of his gun was still on the scene.

Initially, Momo didn't know if it was his friend Quarter or his former schoolmate Abdul who had been shot. All Momo could think about was that he was on bond for some unrelated cases and this shit could land him in jail without bond until trial, which could be a year or two. Momo didn't give a shit about Quarter and didn't care to know if he were alive or dead. All Momo cared about was himself and that's how he acted.

I've known people like Momo my whole life. The Momos of the world manage to play gangster until some gangster shit goes down. Amazingly they are able to convince others to participate and volunteer in their shit. However, it is the volunteer that ends up getting fucked up. Likewise, the Momo's of the world end up signifying how fucked up the shit was; the fucked up shit that they started.

In August of 2008, that's what happened to Quarter. Momo called Quarter to take a run with him. Momo knew that like most nineteen year old pseudo rappers, they'll do anything for a little change and street credibility. I don't know if Momo told Quarter that the kilo he was to sell was flex a/k/a fake cocaine. I don't know if Quarter was only to be present if Momo needed some help as an enforcer if some shit kicked off. However, when Momo got to the location of the sale, he immediately recognized there was a problem. Momo and Abdul grew up together as classmates in high school. Momo had agreed to sell the kilo to Haseem. He didn't know that Abdul would be there. Momo knew that he could not sell this bad dope to someone he knows, so he decided to let Quarter sell it.

Momo suggested that Quarter accompany Abdul and Haseem to their car. Quarter jumped in the backseat behind the driver, Haseem. Abdul was the front seat passenger. After Haseem saw that the dope was flex he reneged on the deal. Quarter became upset because no deal means no money for him. So, Quarter decided to rob Haseem and Abdul, when Abdul shot Quarter in the neck with a .40 caliber automatic gun. The back door opened, when Quarter fell on to the street and was left for dead. When homicide detectives arrived, they found the flex and the magazine to an automatic weapon underneath Quarter's body. The gun it belonged to was gone.

Front Bump a friend of Quarter and Momo just happened to be in the area. Front Bump told police that he saw Quarter lying out in the street so he tried to help. Front Bump picked up Quarter's body and attempted to rush him to the hospital before he encountered the police. The police then took possession of Quarter's limp body and rushed him to the county hospital. Thereafter, police took Front Bump to headquarters for questioning.

Front Bump admitted that Quarter was like a brother to him. He said that he was called to the area by Quarter, but didn't know why. However, police found a .9mm in Front Bump's car.

From the looks of things, Momo had set up a deal to sell fake drugs that turned into an attempted robbery, but ended with Quarter being shot in the neck. For a full thirty days, Momo could not be found as Quarter clinged to life unable to breathe on his own as Homicide Detectives readied themselves for his inevitable death. Police crowded around and crowed to the sedated neck braced Quarter asking him to blink twice if he recognized any of the usual suspects' photos they placed in his face.

To the contrary, Quarter lived. He's paralyzed from the neck down and shits in a bag if not diapers, but he lived. Now, Abdul and Haseem are charged with the attempted murder of Quarter. The state's star witness is Momo, who eventually came forward with his lawyer in tow. The guy that set the whole thing up now wants to seek some justice for his friend, but he doesn't want to be charged with anything claiming to be just a witness.

I knew Momo's lawyer from his days in the District Attorney's Office. Just from looking at him one could glean that he liked product himself. He was of Polish decent and sported a tube of mousse in his dark black hair. Severe acne littered his face, I suspect from his use. Now he's a defense lawyer with a pierced tongue and earrings everywhere. He sports demonic looking rings that only a devil worshiper would wear. I guess his masquerade was a part of a life he had suppressed for a long time. As criminal defense attorneys we're known to be a little different anyway. So, he thinks he can get away with sporting all of this satanic shit. In his self-absorption, he doesn't know that his colleagues look at him like he's crazy as hell. Perhaps, like me, at this point in his life he can care less what others think.

However, one day I was sitting in a jury room where attorneys were assigned to plea bargain their respective cases when Momo's lawyer asked me how the case was going. I told him my version of things before he told me that Momo had stolen his gun from his law office.

Even more, Momo had used his gun in the shoot out with Abdul. What? Then he said, Momo called him from the scene when the shit was going down. He demanded that Momo return his gun that night.

I knew that Momo's lawyer felt comfortable enough with me to even have such a conversation. However, he didn't expect for me to hold him to it. When I told him I would, he promised to assert his attorney client privilege. On the other hand, I didn't give a shit what he was going to do. I had to do what was best for Abdul and I did.

When Quarter was shot, Momo had told the court that neither he nor Quarter had guns. Thus, either Momo lied to the court or his lawyer just made himself a witness in Abdul's case. At any rate, Momo's lawyer could have been lying to me about his gun. But, who would do that? In looking at him, my bet is he traded his gun to Momo for some blow. Still yet, if his gun was at the scene I couldn't let the disclosure slide.

The first time I laid eyes on Abdul, I liked him. Abdul was barely twenty-two years old, a college student who hailed from North Philly, but was reared here in Atlanta. As we conversed, it didn't take long to find out that Abdul was a jazzman. He had been schooled in the straight bass and had been known to sit in on gigs, when other musicians needed him. Abdul being a jazzman and college student accused of attempted murder had me puzzled. I wanted to know what was going on in Abdul's life that triggered him to be a part of this thing. I wanted to know if there was a stressor that took Abdul over the top because this was out of character.

I knew Abdul had a story, but getting him to share it with me was another thing. He needed to trust me and I allowed him to. Abdul was the younger of two kids. He had an older sister who was married to an Assistant District Attorney in Philly, but appeared to have kept her distance from Abdul and the family. Abdul Sr. was a slender, yet tall man. He had a fair complexion, communicative, yet a quiet reserved man. Retired, Abdul Sr. had worked a career in IT. I could tell he was a drinker and I soon found out why after I met his wife.

Abdul's mother was a looker in her day. She had a fair complexion, full lips and curvaceous hips. She was a teacher but she suffered from Attention Deficit Disorder in that she would have her next question ready before she could digest the answer to her first question. As I counseled the family, every time Abdul Sr. opened his mouth his wife would scream at him with uncontrollable rage. I felt sorry for him. Abdul Sr. would keep his cool, however this coolness seemed to inflame her even more.

Abdul Jr. kept his eyes on me even as he attempted to be the peacemaker. So, I kept my eyes on him. I showed him my eyes of understanding because I wanted him to know that I was cool with him and that things were okay. I counseled with his family for over an hour before they left. His mom doubled back as Abdul and his father exited my office. She apologized for her behavior. She then told me that she recently found out that her husband of nearly thirty years was gay. She told me that the hurt and pain of this consumed her. Moreover, she believed that their constant fighting triggered Abdul to go and do something stupid.

Quarter was only nineteen years old when he lost the use of his body. Like many kids his age, he wanted to be a rapper. The word on the street was that he was pretty good. Abdul and Quarter had never met before these events caused a physical and emotional chain reaction. I thought it ironic that both Abdul and Quarter were products of the public school system; neither had prior brushes with the law and both had a passion for music.

Funny how things work out, Haseem brought Abdul and Momo brought Quarter to the drug deal. Neither Quarter nor Abdul woke up that morning expecting to be a part of a drug deal that would change their life forever. But, it did and it didn't take much to get them involved. Thus, I knew something was wrong with that picture too.

I don't know what motivated Quarter to ride with Momo. Some rappers erroneously believe that crime is a Passover into a credible rap career. To rap about the pain and suffering they have inflicted on others somehow leads to validation and street credibility. This idiotic attitude gained momentum from the fools that produce this music to the kid eager to show himself approved. Today, Quarter's rap career is over and his momma's back is fucked up lifting his ass up to change his diaper. Moreover, Quarter's momma adamantly blames Abdul for Quarter's condition and thinks that Abdul should pay for the help needed for a stay at home nurse.

The case was pending for over three years. However, Quarter's father never appeared in court to support his son. I don't know if his dad was dead, but he never showed or any man of a parental figure for that matter. Sometimes, when I see these dynamics, I rhetorically ask myself if there was a man around and if not, why not. In my cornered thinking, I assumed that a man would make things just a little bit better.

To the contrary, Abdul's momma thinks Abdul shouldn't pay anything because Quarter not only tried to sell some fake drugs, which is essentially stealing. When that failed, Quarter at gunpoint tried to rob Abdul and Haseem, when Haseem refused to buy. Sadly, neither Abdul's nor Quarter's momma acknowledged that their boys were involved in a drug transaction when this shit went down. Neither mom wanted to admit that their sons did not have clean hands and should be held responsible for their own circumstances. Whether one should be sent to prison and the other spend his life in purgatory as one suffers from paralysis.

Abdul is now confronted with the idea of his life being a lie. The reality that daddy isn't who he thought he was. All the years of trying to be like dad are now called into question. Suddenly, the fact that he stayed around until your senior year in college and provided for you ain't enough. Sadly, even the sustaining love that he has for you is not enough. Now, you question your sexual orientation as if it's something genetically transferable. Abdul thinks that his dad's sexuality somehow now emasculates his own. To prove himself a man, Abdul decided to do something he thought would validate the reason he has a dick in the first place.

Yeah, I'll carry another man's gun to another man's drug transaction. I will ride and offer assistance for free just because you caught me on the day my mother and father argued again over his sexuality. I'll do this transaction with you in my need to self-evaluate. I'm now on a journey to find out who I am and perhaps crime validates me. In crime, I can prove to myself that I have more thug in me than bitch. Absent this moment in crime, I may have to walk around just a little bit longer before I realize that crime doesn't offer me the peace of mine I so desperately seek. But, I'm so young and immature; I don't realize that in time all things are revealed.

On the eve of trial, the District Attorney came around to believe that Quarter did have a gun when Abdul shot him. I believe the District Attorney observed the raunchy nature of Momo and his attorney and in her heart she didn't believe them. The magazine clip dipped in Quarter's blood found next to the fake drugs only confirmed her suspicion of their truth.

The gun Abdul used was recovered by police and taken as evidence. Moreover, why was Front Bump over in the area of the transaction? Likewise, how did he happen upon Quarter's limp body after he was shot before anyone else? Front Bump's .9mm was found in his car loaded and otherwise intact. Front Bump told police that Quarter told him to meet him at that location because he needed a ride. The District Attorney knew that only those familiar with the deal knew where to come. On the night in question, Haseem and Momo had changed the locations for the deal a few times.

Of the guns recovered from Front Bump and Abdul, the magazine recovered with Quarter's blood on it didn't match either gun. Thus, there was a third gun near or around Haseem's car that could have been used by Quarter. The District Attorney offered Abdul probation for Quarter's attempted murder. I think she only did that to help out Quarter with some medical bills. Abdul took the offer over the objection of Quarter's momma, who still complained about her back was hurting. The charges against Haseem were dismissed.

I told Quarter's momma, but for the grace of God I would be standing here with Quarter and Abdul would be in diapers sitting in that wheel chair. I told her that no one involved in this case had clean hands. She abruptly left the courtroom in resentment of my observations. I know she heard me.

Ironically, Momo and Haseem, whose drug deal it was that forever affected the life of their friends walked away from punishment. Friends, where do the lines begin or end? However, it is my hope that all of these young men remember what happened that night and remember to keep their hands clean. I know they won't. Momo has two pending cases where he's accused of pulling a gun on folks after Quarter was shot. Within months after the case, word has it that Momo's attorney was later arrested in an undercover drug transaction by Atlanta Police. Thereafter, his attorney went to rehab and was subsequently disbarred. The Assistant District Attorney that handled the case was fired.

Sentence: *Plea bargain to attempted murder ten years probation.*

CHAPTER SIX

NEW ORLEANS

WHO KILLED SKINNY PIMP

D yke Red was accused of putting a "hit" on Skinny Pimp over drug turf. To the contrary, Dyke Red wanted Skinny Pimp dead because he pimp smacked her right there on Peachtree Street in front of everybody. Dyke Red had confronted Skinny Pimp before about selling crack on her corner at a reduced price. But things didn't get ugly until Skinny Pimp smacked her. Dyke Red traded sacks of crack cocaine for a cheap gun and gave it to Lamar. There was nothing remarkable about Lamar other than the fact that he was a crack head who would sell himself sexually for some crack. So for a few shacks of crack cocaine, Lamar shot and killed Skinny Pimp.

It's not uncommon for women to murder. Usually, they are very skillful in getting someone else to do it or carry out the deed in exchange for money or sex. Dahlia, Cleopatra, Jean Harris and the black widow are all historic examples of women that murdered men or participated on some level. My college girl, graduate student, Michelle Gudeaux, an evacuee from New Orleans only twenty seven years old was arrested and charged for the murder of Skinny Pimp. Someone "had not so" mistakenly identified her as the person known to them as Dyke Red.

I got a call from a judge that's a friend of mine. The judge was concerned that the state was about to prosecute the wrong person for murder. In his brief interview with Michelle, the judge learned that she was a college girl who had relocated to Atlanta as a result of

Katrina and was allowed to enroll in college here as a courtesy until her university rebuilds. Michelle also had a sister that attended the revered Spelman College that is located here in Atlanta. However, she was here before the hurricane.

When I spoke to Michelle's mom, I knew that they obviously did not have much money so I cut my attorney's fees. I wanted to do my part in what everyone believed to be a travesty of justice waiting to happen. Momma promised me that she would do everything she could to pay me. She told me that when she received her FEMA check, she would pay the balance of the retainer. Michelle's father called me and professed his daughter's innocence. I believed that Michelle was, in fact, the wrong person charged with the murder of Skinny Pimp so I decided to help.

I immediately jumped on the case. I had Michelle's parents send me all of her bank, school and rental history records. Upon receipt and inspection of the records, they all indicated that Michelle was in New Orleans hours before and after the murder of Skinny Pimp. At minimum, I knew that Michelle was not a person that was familiar with the lower side of downtown Atlanta where Skinny Pimp was killed. Nonetheless, the prosecutor was adamant about his belief that Michelle was Dyke Red. Even, if, she did use her debit card at Popeye's Chicken outside the French Quarters hours before the murder, she had time to drive to Atlanta, kill Skinny Pimp and flee back to New Orleans. As silly as it was that was the District Attorney's theory.

I had learned that the guy that identified Michelle to police was in jail. When I attempted to question him about Michelle, it was obvious to me that he was lying. I know enough about people to know when they are positioning themselves to sell information to police. Sadly, this dude was in the business of information exchange for reduced time. I asked him how could he do that? How could he sleep at night? He told me to go fuck myself. I knew he wasn't from Georgia. He had no conscious. Seemingly, it was either his ass or Michelle's and he wasn't crying about someone he didn't know or gave a fuck about. When I visited the other inmate, he told me he knew Dyke Red and Michelle wasn't her. I had the judge produce him in court and they did, he told the judge that Michelle was not Dyke Red. The judge gave Michelle a bond based on the information I had given him.

Michelle was this petite lady with a heavy New Orleans accent that made her beautiful. She was only four feet tall, 90 pounds soaking wet, but she had a nice ass. She wore her hair cut short in a natural style. She had an onion-shaped head and a smile that would make her seem unsure of herself. She was attractive and a lesbian, but not a killer.

When I got Michelle out of jail on bond, she would stop by the office unannounced acting all familiar. In checking out her criminal background, I had learned that Michelle had been involved in a few domestic altercations with women since she had arrived in Atlanta and that's how the police obtained a mug shot of her. One of Michelle's altercations involved a roommate who was dating a lady named Karen. Ironically, I had been out with Karen a few times. Karen and my brother had worked in the same hair salon downtown. At the time, I didn't know that Karen was a lesbian, but she eventually confessed.

Afterwards, Karen said that she could be long-term with me. But after I found out about Karen in the streets, I could never trust her since our friendship was based on deception. Karen told me that she just didn't go around telling people about her sexuality. I understood her point, but I still felt like I had been lied to given the time we had spent together. If she had just told me, she would not have been the first lesbian or sexually ambiguous woman I ever dated. I never told Karen or Michelle about our connection.

As Michelle explained things to me, it was weird at times because she could not account for her whereabouts during the time that Skinny Pimp was killed. The more I pressed her, the more stuff she had forgotten. After her bank statement showed that on the night of the murder, she went to Popeye's in New Orleans, why couldn't she account for herself for the rest of the evening? I asked her when police told her she was being charged with murder, why did she not ask, "Who was killed or where did it happen?" When Michelle was arrested at her apartment and charged with murder, all she said was "wow." I wondered why that was the only thing she said. She asked me, "What the hell should I have said?" I guess I don't know, but I would have started with, it wasn't me.

I began to see that Michelle was under so much stress that she was probably suffering from post-traumatic stress syndrome. I say that because her family had lost everything in the hurricane. The grandmother who helped raise her was gravely ill; her parents were divorcing; the computer store where she had worked prior to her arrest fired her and she was charged with murder. Moreover, she did not know anyone involved in the death of Skinny Pimp or the witnesses that had identified her mug shot to police.

The prosecutor was one of those that seemed to believe that everyone charged with a crime was guilty of something. I knew the type when I work as a prosecutor in Chicago. I knew that I didn't want to be a cowboy like that even though I loved wearing boots. Also, I've always been suspicious of the system and those who work within it. For them, it much easier to become a team player as opposed to an independent thinker. This prosecutor remained adamant about prosecuting Michelle. Even after a hearing, outside the presence of the jury, the co-defendant Lamar testified that he knew Dyke Red very well and Michelle was not Dyke Red.

When we began to strike the jury, Michelle came to court with an older lady that called herself a preacher. I knew the preacher was just a Sugar Momma for Michelle. The Sugar Momma had somehow convinced the church to help pay Michelle's legal fees. I didn't really care where the money came from, so long as I got paid.

At trial, a more experienced prosecutor showed up and became the lead prosecutor. The new prosecutor was a friend of mine; we had attended the same law school in Houston, Texas. While in school, he and I had dated the same married woman that worked at the law school. We still laugh about it when we see each other. The married woman left me for him because I would not allow her to move in with me. I told her that she had a good husband and kids, tough it out. She cussed me out. My friend allowed her and the kids to move in, but I think he benefited from it in many ways.

After we picked the jury, we were into the third witness when the state attempted to call a witness not on the witness list. I objected and the judge allowed a mistrial. About two months went by before we started the trial all over again. By that time, an investigator for the District Attorney's Office found the real Dyke Red. She and Michelle did resemble each other. However, she weighed at least 180 pounds. No exaggeration, she was literally twice the size of Michelle.

The trial was reset again so that the real Dyke Red could get a lawyer. I heard that Michelle testified for the state about her ordeal. I thought it was funny that Michelle didn't call me before she stepped back into the courtroom for the trial. I figured that Michelle just didn't want to see or call me again because she owed me money. Michelle and her mother promised me that they would pay me all of my attorney's fees after she got her FEMA check. Even the Sugar Momma said that if they didn't pay, the church would. To date, I have yet to be paid.

Nonetheless, at least I can sleep at night knowing that I did my part in keeping an innocent person out of prison for the rest of her life. After the trial, Michelle remained in Atlanta. Hopefully, New Orleans can rebuild and we can send everyone who would like to return home. Best wishes.

Sentence: *Dyke Red and Lamar life in prison.*

BLACK

R ico, a New Orleans teenager and Hurricane Katrina transplant was a so-called murder victim after he and a friend went into Black's house to rob him? I thought if he was a victim, then I was the first cousin to the Dali Lama. As Rico entered Black's house with another teenager to rob him, the only thing that changed his mind was that he recognized that there were too many witnesses in the house. During the break-in, the 'Naw Leans teen had cut the phone cords and the power to Black's house before they entered. The robbers were dressed in all black and wearing camouflage coats. They were armed with handguns and used micro flashlights to navigate themselves through the house.

The people of New Orleans showed the rest of the world that what they considered culture, the rest of America considered another excuse for a party. What New Orleans thought of as tradition, America thought of as bad habits and lack of couth. What New Orleans thought of as expectation, America thought of as charity. Seemingly, a thank you America was the least New Orleans could say to those of us that helped you. America didn't want anything in return and she never asks you for your FEMA checks. In the end, America just wanted you to be all right.

Sadly, what left New Orleans were not only her good but also her bad. Her bad, more often than not, became the topic of conversation. They increased the crime rate in Houston, Texas, and Atlanta.

Unfortunately, New Orleans came to Atlanta with her game thinking that her shit was somehow new and different. Some, New Orleaneans had to find out the hard way that shit is shit everywhere you go.

Black was in his early thirties and was running a crack house in the Bluff. The Bluff is one of the most dangerous areas just west of downtown Atlanta. Black told me that he was ready for them as they entered. He could have blasted them right there but he didn't. Black decided not to blast them after he realized that it was this teenager from New Orleans in his house. Instead, Black tried to talk to him and told him how close he came to being shot. Black followed the teenager out of his house for about a block before everything kicked off.

When Black and the teenager made it to the corner of Elm Street, Black saw the teenager's older brother talking with some girls. Black said he guess the nigga got brave when he saw his older brother. At least, that's when the teenager pulled out his gun and tried to shoot Black. Black blasted him. The kid died on the spot. See, the teenager didn't know that as far as Atlanta is concerned, the Bluff is the same in every major city in America. Whether you are in New York City, Baltimore, Philadelphia, Washington, D.C. or the West side of Chicago, where crack is sold. The Bluff in Atlanta is the same.

Black's mother, Rose used to work for me as a bill collector. Rose hired me to represent Black for Rico's murder. Rose was surprised when I quoted her my regular fee. She said, "I thought I was family?" I told that she was, but I didn't know her son. Rose said so I have to go kill somebody to get the family rate. I said something like that. We laughed before I reduced the charge to the family rate. Her old man was shitty that Rose was paying Black's legal fees. As a child, Rose never raised Black. I think she felt kind of guilty about that and this time she wanted to help.

However, when Rose's new husband continued to complain. Rose backed off paying me. Thereafter, Rose introduced me to her daughter who worked as a stripper. I didn't fuck her but I would have. I just wanted my money. I began to complain. Eventually, Rose gave into the pressure and died. I believe that Rose killed herself. Somehow, Rose had overdosed on some prescription medication. Sadly, this was the second time I had to go to the County Jail and tell a client that his mother had died. It wasn't any easier.

At trial, the folks in the house with Black testified about the blackout and then the burglary. A friend of Rico's even testified about the gun that someone removed from Rico's person after he was killed and hid it in her home. The entire country was talking about how tired they were of some folks from New Orleans wreaking havoc in their schools and communities. Atlanta was no different. This was my fourth case involving a homicide where someone from New Orleans here as a result of Hurricane Katrina was involved.

America was in denial that such a disaster could happen and she not be prepared. America's denial became anger. She was angry with herself because of her response or lack thereof. Frustrated by her own incompetence, America became disappointed with her president and the government. It took some time but in her resilience, America turned her depression into charity to try to show some Christian love. America attempted to bargain off her grief through giving.

After the water dried up, America started to take a closer look at New Orleans. America opined that New Orleans had allowed herself to become vulnerable because she didn't take care of her own house. It started when she neglected her infrastructure and waited on the Army Corp of Engineers to advise them. New Orleans had neglected to diversify her economy to bring in new and different revenue streams into the city. For years, New Orleans was satisfied with just blaming the state of Louisiana for most of her problems. Sadly, New Orleans never did anything to work on her thick accent, which made it difficult for natives to explain themselves to the world. Eventually, the rest of America just looked at folks from New Orleans as ungrateful and accepted that as a fact. An American Government led by a man whose own mother thought that people sleeping in an old dome in Houston, Texas were better off than before the hurricane. Even if she were correct in her opinion, the fact that she said it was condescending and in poor taste.

The jury found Black guilty of voluntary manslaughter. For me, that was a win because we beat the life sentence for a murder conviction. So I'm thinking Black will be paroled one day and not spend the rest of his life in prison. Much to my surprise, the judge threw the book at Black. The judge reasoned that because Black followed the teenager for more than a block, Black had time to calm down and call police. Much to the court's chagrin, I told the judge that he had missed the point the jury tried to make, which was they acknowledged that Black tried to save a life before he had to defend his own. Ironically, if Black had just shot the kid in his house, Black probably would not have spent one day in jail. Conversely, I don't think Black will ever get out.

Sentence: *Voluntary manslaughter twenty years for Rico's death and a consecutive twenty years for aggravated assault against Rico's brother.*

BIRTHDAY WISHES

A ll rise, the Clerk of Court announced that the jury had a question. Before the court could assemble the lawyers and return the defendant to the table. The bailiff returned and informed us that the jury had a verdict. I knew I was entitled to at least read the jury's question. But, at the time it seemed rather irrelevant. They had worked it out. Everyone paused and waited on the jury to re-enter the court room.

As I waited, I began to reminisce about New Orleans and when my love for her began. The food, music and culture were something that was different for an Indiana boy like me. Being Up-Town in New Orleans reminded me of pictures I had seen of Paris. As we collectively waited on the jury, my mind began to wander with random thoughts of my life, birthplace and New Orleans.

I thought to myself it's funny how one place can be the center of your universe. For others, they hardly know that your universe exists. As a college kid, I was shocked when a college friend told me that he didn't know there were black folks in Indianapolis. He thought that all blacks from Indiana were from Gary. On the contrary, blacks in Indianapolis thought that they were socially and morally better than blacks from Gary. Blacks in Indianapolis thought that blacks from Gary were wild and uncivilized. The blacks in Gary were just imitating the behavior of blacks just over the bridge in Chicago.

New Orleans was something much better than anything I had ever seen. A cultural experience unlike anywhere in America, she stood alone. New Orleans before Las Vegas was a middle class destination. People around the world knew the pedigree of New Orleans musicians were unparallel because of Sachmo, Terrence Blanchard, Reginald Veal and the Marsalis brothers. As a law student, I thought that they were so cool and unassuming when they would take time to visit with their childhood friend, my ex-wife when they were in town. New Orleans was an education in race, customs and individuality. At least, that's what she used to be until something changed.

I don't know what occurred to make New Orleans change but it did and I didn't like it. At some point, the accent I once thought of as sexy annoyed me. I didn't like the lazier fair or attitude of indifference of its people toward life. Seemingly, the rest of the world didn't matter to the native New Orleanian until she needed help. In spite of her conceited attitude America eventually helped her. In the process, America had to bring her distant cousin in to her home while she began to rebuild her city. For the first time, America saw how narrow, emotional and mentally handicapped people can become when they isolate themselves from the rest of America or when America isolates one of her own.

Over the years New Orleans had trivialized herself when she continued to be known as a party girl. She was known as someone to hang out with but not take home to momma. Consequently, matters of local government and its sustainability fell by the wayside. The Federal and State Governments began to ignore New Orleans as the unwanted girl after she refused to keep herself up.

To the contrary, Indianapolis never isolated herself from America. Its people were just disenfranchised when the manufacturing and automakers closed shop. The federal money given to help out was used to make what was a little decent better. Thus, federal money never made it to my community in Indianapolis. But, in the 1980's the Baltimore Colts did and that made all the difference in the world. The city used the federal money and ran Highway 70 right in the heart of my neighborhood. The unused portion was taken by the Indianapolis Colts. Eventually, the city will take the rest of my neighborhood under their eminent domain powers. Thereafter, my trip back home will surely be nostalgic. My parents are long deceased and with no family home to return to all I have are the memories.

The lack of federal funds flowing into my neighborhood kept us poor but not broke. Growing up without a shower or bath tub almost seemed un-American to me. The Board of Health never condemned our home. As a child, pictures of abject poverty in the Appalachian and rural south only encouraged me to keep my secret that I was a step away. We were poor but we had this magical faith woven together by love. As a child, the abundant love I received still sustains me.

Today, as I sit here in my designer suit, necktie and Gucci shoes. I stared at Dishman like he's from outer space. He's my client from New Orleans. He's at the table waiting with me to see if the jury will convict him of murder. The bailiff announced to the court that the jury was present and assembled. The judge instructed us to be seated and in the same breath she began to communicate with the jury. "I understand that you've reached a verdict?" The foreperson stood and replied "We do your honor".

Dishman was accused of shooting Darius Miles, a thieving crack head over thirty dollars worth of Ecstasy pills. Consistent with the street logic indigenous to the ghetto, it wasn't the amount of drugs involved but the perceived disrespect in not paying the debt on time. The macho attitude of being taken advantage of however slight warrants the violence. This macho attitude has been drilled in young urban black men from birth. He will demand respect from his people even though those in the larger community ignores him, if they see him at all. To the contrary, the invisible man will not be disrespected or ignored by a street urchin much like himself.

Witnesses stated that the shooter shot Darius in the back. As Darius fell to the ground, the shooter stood over him and shot him again in the face and chest. One of the bullets passed through Darius' heart. The Medical Examiner surmised that if the wound to the heart didn't kill him the one to the face certainly did. Witnesses heard the shooter say in a very heavy New Orleans accent, "That's what you get for stealing," before he fled. Police started looking for Dishman after Edward a homeless crack head told police he saw Dishman shoot Darius.

Edward, whose street name ironically is "N.O.", short for New Orleans because of his heavy accent was the state's star witness. He never told police that he was the driver of the getaway car. However, he did tell police that he was the person that brought Darius family to the crime scene. Also, he was the first to tell the family that Darius had been shot. Sadly, Darius mother and brother saw Darius dead body sprawled out on the apartment complex parking lot.

I hope to never know how it feels to see a loved one sprawled out in the streets or anywhere for that matter covered by the white sheet reserved for the dead. As cops stand by drinking coffee and smoking cigarettes as they discuss last night's game and family matters incidental to the homicide they're now investigating. I hope to never know how it feels to lose a child. Day in and day out, I pray that a kid that finds himself in an imaginary wronged situation gives in to humanity. I hope that he allows his trespasser to live.

I knew that "N.O." was lying when he told police that he just happened to be there when Darius was shot. So, here I am again trying to explain the slick shit people do to the uniformed. I needed to explain how people do and say shit to deflect attention away from themselves. "N.O." was about 6 feet tall and crack head skinny. He adorned a dull black complexion and stained rotten teeth from his habitual drug use. Like most crack heads, I knew the truth wasn't in him and if it was, you had to pay for it.

Witnesses identified "N.O." as the driver of the getaway car when he returned to the scene with Darius' family. Also, a witness identified "N.O." as the person with Darius when he banged on her neighbor's door. The witness claimed that Darius banged on the door so hard the pictures fell from her wall. Like most crack heads, "N.O." story changed after police confronted him with the witness identification of him before, during and after the shooting. As police turned up the heat on "N.O.," he began to tell police about the thirty dollars worth of pills Darius was given to sell on consignment from Dishman.

This wasn't my first experience with a crack head. I've known a crack head in every city I've ever worked in. Some of my friends and family members have become crack heads. Based on my personal and professional experience, I'm adept at dealing with lying ass crack heads. I knew that I had to strike the crack head first before he could control me. I mean it's virtually impossible to out talk a crack head because they think they know every damn thing.

So it's imperative to control him and the conversation. For example, if you're ever approached by a crack head for money be sure to ask them first. Certainly, they will cry broke and admit that they were just about to ask you for money. Before, the crack head realizes that you struck first, you would have left the scene or changed the conversation leaving the crack head to ponder what just happened.

Duke Greasy hired me to represent Dishman. I knew who Duke was when he pulled out thousands of dollars in small denominations to pay Dishman's retainer fees. Duke weighed over 300 pounds and sported an oversized tee shirt, jeans and Air Jordan gym shoes. People will claim to be good friends until money gets involved. However, an employer will do most anything for a good employee. The good employee may be a good earner and otherwise profitable. Duke paid me in cash and I thanked him for it.

As with many clients that pay me in full they look at me as if to say, I've done my part now go do yours. To them, it doesn't matter how bad the facts are or who killed whom and why. It's always the same, get my guy off. Remarkably, I try very hard to do just that. It never matters how bad the facts are I always think I can win. At least, that's what I'll keep telling myself until I believe it. Just like an aging athlete who still thinks he can play failing to realize he's not what he used to be.

Dishman was in his late twenties and stood about 5'9". He had a medium brown bag complexion with darker colored life marks and scares about his face. He was not confident in his ability to communicate with me or others. His New Orleans accent played heavy on his vowels and he ended each word like a crescendo. He never really initiated conversation and was agreeable with my perception of things. Also, I found him to piggy back off comments made by me not offering an original thought or opinion of his own. He had been set free by New Orleans authorities on a murder. The files had been lost or misplaced during the hurricane. He was being investigated for another murder in Atlanta that involved a beef over drug territory.

The only time we shared a moment was when he told me about his Hurricane Katrina story of survival. He and his twenty-seven year old, five hundred pound cousin had to steal an eighteen wheeler to flee New Orleans as stranded evacuees. Without the medical necessities for diabetes, Dishman told me they did what they had to do. They made it safely to Baton Rouge but remained anonymous for two weeks before they were found by family members in Houston. Dishman confided in me that it was hard to keep his cousin fed.

I saw Dishman as a man that had love in his heart as he explained how his cousin became his friend. He explained how lonely it can be if you don't have anyone to talk to that understands where you're coming from. Dishman told me that he loved his momma and that he gets his big heart from her. She's a cancer survivor. A few years ago, Dishman's cousin died on Dishman's birthday. Dishman uses his birthday to mourn the death of his cousin and friend. But now, the trial is over and the jury has spoken. The judge directed the foreperson to stand and read the verdict. Dishman has another reason not to celebrate his birthday.

Sentence: *Life*

FACES I HAVE SEEN

ABOUT THE AUTHOR

Ted Johnson has a successful career as a criminal defense lawyer and is originally from Indianapolis, Indiana. He attended Rice University and Thurgood Marshall School of Law, before moving to Chicago in 1989. He then trained as a prosecutor in the Cook County State Attorney's Office before moving to Atlanta, Georgia in 1993. In Atlanta, he began his criminal defense career and became a public defender. In 1996, he started his law firm and entered into private practice. He still resides in the Atlanta area.

www.ingramcontent.com/pod-product-compliance
Lightning Source LLC
Chambersburg PA
CBHW032000170526
45157CB00002B/472